# ImagiNation

Stories of Scotland's Future

Aberdeens....

# ImagiNation

## Stories of Scotland's Future

Edited by
Bryan Beattie and Gerry Hassan

Big Sky Press

First published in 2011
by Big Sky Press
www.big-sky.co
Big Sky Press is an imprint of
Creative Services (Scotland) Ltd, Drumderfit, North Kessock, IV1 3ZF

Frontispiece illustration by David Tomei.

ISBN 978-0-9569578-0-1

Printed and bound in Poland, EU by Totem, Bookwork PL.

# Contents

# Contents

# Preface

Not long after starting the journey to create this book we came across James Robertson's essay, Who Are The Scots?, in *The Sunday Herald*. Although we intended to produce an anthology of fiction, James' words seemed to echo the essence of what we wanted to capture.

In the essay James paints a compelling picture of the life-journey we travel – individual or country – and the incremental changes that shape us, unnoticed until we stop, look back, and see 'a new ship built on an old plank'.

The brief to the writers in this collection was to make their story the end point of such a journey – to imagine Scotland weeks, months or years into the future and describe what they see, and to hint at the values that have shaped this imagined country of the future.

As the project's originator, Gerry Hassan's concluding essay provides an appropriate 'bookend' to the fictional pieces, providing broader context for story in Scotland, and neatly anticipating the planned companion volume to this anthology.

It has been a privilege to work on this book with so many wonderful imaginations in Scotland, from the weel-kent to those making their first appearance in print in this anthology; and a particular pleasure to see writers from comic book, drama, poetry and short story sit alongside each other.

It's also a wonderful collection with which to launch a new publisher in Scotland – Big Sky Press. With luck, as we drift down James Robertson's metaphorical river, we will have the chance to publish more of the work of these and other writers in future years. We look forward to the journey.

Bryan Beattie
Big Sky Press

# Welcome to ImagiNation

We know we need a new story for Scotland. The writers in this book have started to explore what that might be. Sometimes it will look not too much different from the way it did yesterday (like the characters in our playwrights' ensemble piece, *Welcome to Hotel Caledonia*), and at other times it will be as distant a land as Kirsty Logan's *One Hundred Years of Wifehood* seems to us now.

We can all recognise the world painted by Alan Warner's *It All Falls Down Like Silver* (though we may not want to live next door to it) or Ronald Frame's *Borrowed Landscape*, a wonderful extended metaphor that sums up the desire to widen our vision beyond what is 'owned' by us, to embrace the shared beauty and opportunity open to all humanity.

Maybe Scotland's story *is* changing and the stories in this book are evidence of it? *Luvvable 'Lex* has the power and redemptive possibilities of love at his core even although the exterior is a bit grim and horrible. Bill Duncan's wonderfully idiosyncratic *Seachurch* is peppered with ecstasy (the divine kind). Raman Mundair breathes hope into despair in her *The Fàilte Policy*. Even Sam Irving's Caledonian Howl, *Naeb'dy's Chiel*, ends on a note of sunshine.

Is the wheel turning? Have we, like James Robertson's introductory essay suggests, renewed all our country's various body parts over time so that it looks the same but is actually different, completely re-made?

Our own life stories are unique and part of a wider collective experience that touches on what makes us human. This was one of the reasons I was enthusiastic to develop the potential of the national A Scottish Wave of Change project, of which this book is one small but significant part.

A Scottish Wave of Change (the project) is like *ImagiNation* (the book it spawned) – filled with hope, optimism, creativeness, fuzziness and invention in the best senses of all these words. It starts from the idea of the power of stories at an individual, collective, societal and national level. It recognises the numerous levels that story operates on, what they say about us, who speaks and doesn't speak, the stories that come to the fore, the hidden stories, and how accounts change across time and history.

This book brings together a rich variety of Scottish voices imagining Scotland's future, some famous, some emerging, all talented, fascinating and thoughtful, and telling us something about ourselves. We offer this book about our future at a fascinating time in our country, a time which seems to offer the prospect of significant and far-reaching change, and which seems to be characterised by a sense of opening, hope and liberation. The new story of modern Scotland has already begun and this book and the authors in it are part of that process.

Gerry Hassan
A Scottish Wave of Change

# THE CURIOUS TIME-PIECE OF SCOTTISH IDENTITY

## James Robertson

You look at a photograph of yourself as a child. You remember when and where it was taken, perhaps what the weather was like or what happened next. The location may be much changed, or it may be just as it was; you may even still return there from time to time, but one thing is certain – the child in the picture has gone for ever. You remember so clearly – or think you do – the blue bicycle, the rope swing, the grazed knee, or the salty cold bite of the sea, but the child is away. And what of all the minutes and hours and years that have passed between the moment of that photograph and the present moment of looking at it? What happened to *them*?

My mother sent me a birthday card a couple of years ago: 'Is it really fifty years since you joined us?' she wrote, and I was completely disarmed by the question. It was indeed astonishing that the time had gone so fast, but there seemed to be only the most tenuous of links between my arrival and the present. The past exists in my memory like a mass of post-its stuck on a notice-board, a multi-coloured melee of unrelated incidents, but between me and that board there is an uncrossable space. To lessen the chaos of the messages it displays, I need to construct a narrative, a chronological frame-work, between it and me, then and now. Clichés are useful: 'the story so far', 'the book of life', 'a new chapter opens'. But still, after all, the gap remains. I am no longer whoever I once was.

'People say that the whole human frame in all its parts and divisions is gradually in the act of decaying and renewing,' Sir Walter Scott reflected in his journal on the first day of 1826. 'What a curious time-piece it would be that could indicate to us the moment this gradual and insensible change had so completely taken place that no atom was left of the original person who had existed at a certain period but there existed in his stead another person having the same limbs, thewes and sinews, the same face and lineaments, the same consciousness – a new ship built on an old plank... Singular – to be at once another and the same.'

That the turn of any year should provoke such thoughts is not surprising, but the difference between the Scott of 1825 and the Scott of 1826 would prove to be dramatic. 1826 would be his *annus horribilis*: before January was out he would know for sure that he was financially ruined; in February he would have to sell his Edinburgh house and sign his affairs over to a trust; in May his wife would die, and he would resign himself to a future of increasingly lonely drudgery, churning out millions of words to pay off his debts. The old paradox captured in the story of the ship of Theseus – when every timber, rope and sail has been repaired or replaced, can the ship still be said to be the same ship? – applied to him, as it applies to all human beings. The child becomes the adult, but is the adult really the same being as the child?

Scott indulged in such musings often, and not only in relation to his own life. He wondered too about the continuing identity of his country. In 1814, in a postscript to *Waverley*, his massively successful, ground-breaking novel of the Jacobite Rising of 1745, he wrote the following: 'There is no European nation which, within the course of half a century or little more, has undergone so complete a change as this kingdom of Scotland ...' The failure of the '45 had led to the destruction of the Highland clan system and the wholesale reorganisation of dispensation of justice throughout Scotland; this had been followed by commercial, scientific and agricultural innovations, an increase in national and private wealth, and the early stirrings of industrial revolution. 'But the change,' Scott went on, 'though steadily and rapidly progressive, has, nevertheless, been gradual; and, like those who drift down the stream of a deep and smooth river, we are not aware of the progress we have made until we fix our eye on the now distant point from which we have been drifted.'

This is a striking image, and even though the pace of change has increased to a sprint it still rings true. I often thought that my maternal grandfather, who lived to his late nineties, must have looked back on his life almost as if parts of it were a dream: as a child in the very early 1900s he was taken on a miraculous expedition in a 'motor car', from Dundee to Perth and back; he served in the First World War and saw the coming of aeroplanes, tanks, radio, television, atom bombs, space travel, heart transplants and unimaginable social change. 'Unimaginable' is the right word: it is easier to experience such changes than to imagine them. And now I realise that I have inherited the dream. Looking back over the 'half a century or little more' that I have lived, I find that what happened only ten or twenty years ago feels like ancient history. The 1997 General Election, the poll tax, the miners' strike are distant enough; but beyond them lies a country almost exotic in its strangeness, yet strangely familiar. We cannot return there, but it is still ours. It is where we come from.

It is a human trait, and not one exclusive to those of us who make our livelihoods from storytelling, to look back along the paths we have travelled and pick out markers. Stories are what make us; they enable us to make sense of our lives; and so we tell and retell them, consciously and subconsciously, to ourselves – and to others when they will listen – shaping the past so that it fits the present and also the possible or preferred future. Bitterness, happiness, loss, reward, a sense of failure or of achievement – all contribute to the narrative. We omit, we conflate, we over-emphasise some incidents while underplaying others, and some items we consign to the darkest corners of our minds and try to forget their existence altogether. And what we do as individuals, we also do collectively, as communities, societies and nations. Or historians, writers, and sometimes politicians, do it on our behalf. But when they do, what is kept out of sight, what is falsified, what is true and what is up for negotiation?

Walter Scott played this game with astonishing skill and panache, and was motivated to do so by a potent mixture of intellect, passion and prejudice. He defined Scotland through its history, which he retold through poetry and fiction, and because he did not like much of what he saw of the future he tried to fix Scotland in the past, as a kind of adventure playground into which he and his readers could step to escape the fears and worries of whatever was coming next. And for Scott there was no clear boundary between the country of his imagination and the Scotland of reality. On one occasion, the innovations in Scottish law being urged by his more reformist-minded friends so agitated him that when they tried to make light of their differences he was reduced to tears in the street. 'No, no – 'tis no laughing matter,' he told them. 'Little by little, whatever your wishes may be, you will destroy and undermine, until nothing of what makes Scotland Scotland shall remain.' It as if he could see what he loved slipping physically from his hands.

It isn't hard to sympathise with Scott's gut resistance to what he once called a 'disposition to change everything in Scotland to an English model', but his intense patriotism was so closely bound up with his political and social conservatism that in time he came to abhor almost *any* change. This is ironic, because it was Scott's ability to paint a vast canvas depicting individuals caught up in the tides of historical change that made him such a significant and popular writer. He revolutionised the novel, opening up the scope of what fiction as an art-form could do.

The conventional impulse in telling any story, historical or invented, is to get to an end-point. Scotland's story seems especially bestrewn with end-points: the Union of 1707 and the 1745 Rising are the two most obvious. For many years it was widely held that nothing Scottish happened after one or other of these dates. Scott set the tone: '[Nothing has] occurred in Scotland at large to furnish matter for the continuation of these narratives,' he wrote at the end of *Tales of a Grandfather*, his children's history of Scotland, referring to the seventy years between Culloden and the time of writing. There might be the odd spasm – in 1832, say (the year of the Reform Act and of Sir Walter's own demise), or 1843 (the year of the Disruption of the Kirk) – but the Union with England and the rise of the British Empire meant that Scottish history was effectively dead.

This was not – and is not – a peculiarly Unionist point of view. For some Nationalists, Scottish time has continued in suspension since 1707: everything that has happened or will happen between then and the resumption of full independence is a kind of diversion from the true path of our history. If only this interim period could be over, the implication is, we could be properly Scottish again. Yet throughout the last three hundred years 'Scottishness' has never gone away, although it has shape-shifted continuously, not only as society has altered but also as different elements of what it might mean to be Scottish have been championed or exploited for a variety of political and cultural reasons. On the one hand, this should neither surprise nor dismay us: no identity, individual or communal, remains the same. On the other hand, nor should we be surprised by the power that a sense of Scottishness has to inform our opinions on the most banal as well as the most serious of matters. That Scottish national identity is very much 'live currency' is clearly shown by the way arguments over the release of Abdelbaset Mohmed Ali al-Megrahi were coloured by notions of differing Scottish and British interests, perceptions of what constitutes 'Scottish justice', and so forth. The wider continuing debate about the bombing of Pan Am Flight 103, and whether Megrahi was solely responsible for it or himself the victim of an outrageous miscarriage of that same Scottish justice, is also profoundly affected by, and affects, the way many Scots think of their national identity, and the way Scotland is perceived by others.

The truth about all history is that there are no end-points. There never were and never will be. Socialists once dreamed that history would end with the collapse of capitalism. Some right-wing historians actually claimed it *had* ended with the collapse of Communism. For some of those who campaigned for decades for devolution, the re-establishment of a parliament in Edinburgh felt like the end of a journey, whereas in fact it was only a staging-post. Historians and novelists are always tempted by conclusions. They want to tie loose ends up into THE END, bring the story to a close. But the story never is over. And the lives of individuals do not fit neatly within the historical chapters into which, for sanity's sake, we divide the past. Our ragged endings and beginnings do not align with the abolition or re-establishment of parliaments or with the deaths and accessions of sovereigns.

One of the great, unsettling, sceptical truths that came out of the Scottish Enlightenment – the very 'hotbed of genius' that shaped the historically-minded Walter Scott – is contained in James Hutton's statement about geological time in his 'Theory of the Earth': 'The result of our present enquiry is that we find no vestige of a beginning, no prospect of an end.' Writing a novel (*And the Land Lay Still*) about the last half-century of life in Scotland felt a little like that. It was like completing a jigsaw puzzle with no straight edges and no picture on the lid of the box, or with a picture that kept changing as I shuffled the pieces around. The Scotland we inhabit bears only passing resemblance to the Scotland of the 1950s, yet it is the same place. We have drifted so far down the smooth, deep river that we're not even sure we can see where we first embarked. And all that weight of unstoppable water has flowed with us. How do we make our aimless drift into a voyage with any meaning?

Perhaps this is something fiction can do for us. Perhaps fiction can move across and occupy the space between past and present in a way that our separate and collective memories cannot. It seems such an obvious thing to say, but the usefulness, the necessity even, of novels is that they tell us stories that *are* imaginable.

'Stands Scotland where it did?' Resoundingly, no. What happened? Much that we remember, much more that we have forgotten. What will happen next? Who can possibly tell? We are into the second decade of devolution, we have a Nationalist government in Edinburgh soon to be tested at the ballot box, Scottish Labour in apparently robust shape and a Lib-Con coalition in power at Westminster, our banks have destroyed themselves, and the oil is beginning to run out. Whatever is in store for us, it will certainly not be the end of the story.

*Postscript*
I wrote that final paragraph in August 2010. As proof of its last sentence, the Scottish parliamentary election of May 2011 delivered what the

devolutionary electoral system had been carefully designed to make impossible – an overall majority for one party. Even more surprisingly, that party was the SNP. Labour, far from being robust, ran a feckless and complacent campaign and, despite securing almost as many votes as it had in 2007 and 2003, suffered humiliation at the hands of the Nationalists, who swept up vast numbers of disaffected LibDem voters (that party having been tainted by association with the coalition government at Westminster), along with some Tories and former supporters of the Far Left, to ensure a decisive victory. The SNP's combined constituency and regional vote amounted to around forty-five percent of the total votes cast, and the turnout was just over fifty percent, so not everything has changed, and it is much too early to declare, 'We are all Nationalists now'. Nevertheless, the election result – which was truly *un*imaginable even the day before it happened – propels Scotland into the next phase of its story. Sir Walter Scott's remark is worth quoting again: 'Singular – to be at once another and the same.'

The Scots have always been an unhappy people; their history is a varying record of heroism, treachery, persistent bloodshed, perpetual feuds and long-winded and sanguine arguments.

Edwin Muir (1887–1959), *Scottish Journey*

# IT ALL POURS DOWN LIKE SILVER

## Alan Warner

I was the only remaining passenger on the two coach Sprinter train as it moved cautiously into my dark town, beneath the great and ugly mountain. Two hours late because of the snow, not a living thing met the train, except a predatory seagull, standing on a litter bin.

Snow adhered to the front and the train driver was switching off the interior lighting, then he slid the cab door closed as I passed. We were almost in a completed darkness. I hitched my backpack and asked quietly, 'Weren't you and me at the high school together?' My breath made a startlingly thick cloud which I had to squint through.

'Can you move off railway property, please. People have been trying to sleep in the train.' I saw the driver's hand wave me away then grab a big gate, swinging it around, shut. I was forced to take a few steps back – off railway property. I spoke out again, but sensed only the seagull alighting behind me. The train driver had vanished in that gloom.

I then squinted up at the massive mountain, in the direction of the cable-car, where the ski-tows and chair-lift pylons were laced high above the town, but even with flanks of snowfield, all was invisible.

The old Victorian railway station had gone and the replacement looked like a Wimpey Bar.

When I last visited Rasta Angus, John Major was Prime Minister and Angus had been renting one of those two storey, ex-council houses backed onto the canal. When we'd linked up on Facebook, I wasn't surprised to learn that he was still in residence. I could distinguish his front garden amongst the well-tended ones: dead docken leaves and rusted foxgloves, fossilised in ice; three deflated footballs, cradling moulds of frozen snow.

Over the barking and aggressive scuffling, Angus opened the front door just enough not to let his dog out. Its leather muzzle busied with fury at the two inch gap. Angus said, 'Must be fifteen years and you turn up when I haven't done the hoovering.'

'I'll forgive you.'

He undid three chains. The house interior stunk of cat pee, yet it was also extremely cold. In the corridor, holding back his dog, Angus stated, 'Well, hark at us. You don't look like a junkie and I'm not an alkie. What the hell went wrong?'

I chuckled.

'Step onto the estate and wipe your feet on any of the cats.'

The dog was called Aleister Growley. Angus was wearing an incongruous *Monaco* t-shirt, under his leather biker jacket. In the scullery, facing the canal, he asked, 'Cuppa?'

'Aye, please.'

'There's no milk. No fridge. Keep cartons outside but they freeze, or Growley busts them and the cats lap it up. We'll get a can of condensed off Eilidh at the garage.' He repeated, 'Eilidh,' and winked.

I watched him step to the mantelpiece of a disused fireplace and lift a faded greetings card. The caption on the front read, *Have A Drink On Me.* He pulled the tea bag free, dropped it into a mug then threw the card away. As I sipped the very watery infusion, I noted it was a vintage, *Defend the Gains of the Revolution*, Sandinista's mug.

A Persian cat I hadn't noticed, manoeuvred violently, swerved across the kitchen floor and out, fleeing my continued presence. It seemed to run into Growley in the corridor and there was the sound of feline combat.

'Fluff Project 6,' Angus mused, then added, 'I'm glad you're back. Hard to find a good night man these days.'

He gave me a wee tour. My bedroom was to be at the back, facing the canal. There was ice on the inside of the window glass. I could see the canal was completely frozen solid in an unsure, flat pallet of quarter-moonlight.

Angus told me, 'Crust is still too thick on the land. Never known a winter like it.'

'Aye.' I nodded.

'A wee hint of thaw and that'll be us,' he assured me.

He led me back out, onto the landing. When he put the bare bulb on in the bathroom, withered, jelly deodorants were everywhere. The sink, cistern and the bath had been shattered to pieces and the pink fragments mostly removed. All the available floor space was occupied by four or five cat litter trays, needing changed.

'The landlord can't evict me; he came round with a sledgehammer and smashed the bog in. As if that would work. Fascist. I wash in the kitchen sink.'

I frowned. 'How do you ... manage?'

'There's good showers for lorry drivers at wee Eilidh's garage and she's give me the key.' He winked. 'Pee in the bucket there and I'll dump it in the canal at night. When the thaw comes.'

'Aye, but what about? Number twos?'

'What do you think?' He nodded frankly to the cat trays and I saw the roll of loo paper next to one. 'The cats never use mine, snooty devils.'

Fruits of the harvest, Angus had a new laptop on broadband, the latest Xbox and a huge flat-screen telly, bolted to a wall; a neighbour-baiting Dolby cinema sound system lurked behind an imitation leather sofa, where a lair of more cats conspired. Angus ran *Terminator* or *Alien* movies in endless succession. He had an annoying habit of constantly using the word *over*, in a geographically vague way. 'When Don Nix was a producer *over* at Stax records ... No, no. Jim Sillars was *over* at the Labour Party in them days ... I know where you were, you were *over* in Glasgow, shacking up on that student lassie with the legs.'

And then there was, 'My brothers in Africa,' this, and, 'My brothers in Africa,' that. Fair enough. I'm all for liberation. But the farthest I'd ever heard of Angus straying – since the demise of the Glasgow Apollo, was a Stirling weekend in 1989.

Late on, he muted Arnie's one-liners and turned to me with a certain profundity. 'There's something you should know about me.'

'What?' I asked, timorously.

'I'm barred from Tesco.'

'I see.'

Angus told me how he was tired of playing Xbox alone, and suggested *Pro-Evolution Soccer 5*, adding, temptingly, that he'd programmed the Scottish squad to be quite invincible and once thrashed England, eleven-nil in a World Cup final.

I didn't sleep well. Thank goodness for earplugs. And I used my spare set, one jammed up each nostril, as Aleister Growley's leather muzzle snarled ominously all night at the gap beneath my bedroom door.

In the morning, I foolishly walked in bare feet and scattered cat biscuits soon lodged between all my toes. Fluff Project 6 had a tin of cat food completely stuck on its head; it had been rooting in, to lick at the base. The cat ran soundlessly from room to room, impacting the skirting and driving the tin further down, until we cornered her. When I returned to the kitchen,

I stepped in a wet cat turd and screamed. The ginger culprit took off up the chimney, and he didn't come back down either. Hopping, I washed my foot in the kitchen sink. There was frozen water round the plughole.

Bizarrely enough, despite the stench, a puritanical no-smoking policy was in operation, and I had to stand out in the back green while it snowed. I strolled down to the canal edge. Resting on the thick canal ice was an enormous heap of cat litter – I could distinguish feline and human waste, clustered together in small gray gravel.

We listened to the Ski Forecasts. Good conditions prevailed and full pistes for another few days yet. 'Ski Lift Restaurant is open to welcome you with its stunning views.'

Suddenly Angus said, 'Let's go up the town,' exactly as we used to opti-mistically say, every day of our school years. Vengefully, Growley watched us depart through the front window, the glass almost opaque with his frozen slobbers.

Snow ploughs had bundled up such huge sorbets of mud-dyed dykes at the roadsides, the pavements had been obliterated. We had to clamber over the fence, knocking down fifty long feet of snow muffle around the wires, then we covered half a mile in the fields, moving adjacent to the main road with our climbing boots cracking through perma-crust.

'You know what Shell have been up to in Nigeria?' I insinuated, outside the garage.

His face took on a stricken look, but he asked no more. He bought a tin of Carnation milk, laying coins bashfully on the counter.

'What's doing?' the young girl asked.

'Just waited on the thaw, like everyone else, Eilidh,' he replied, truthfully enough.

'I love it. There's hardly no traffic on the roads,' she sneered, in an insur-gent manner.

There were no shops left up the town. Just the giant bunker of Tesco and its car parks, which had somehow got planning permission to cut off the town centre.

'I'm going to sue Tesco. I can take them on. Nearly starved to death when they barred me.'

He winked and nodded at roary-cheeked young women wearing scarves and fleeces, lost in his own inner census-taking operation. I became quite inured to his nudges and winks. Alarmingly, at each pub we passed, he'd stated, 'I'm barred from there. There too.'

We entered the only establishments it appeared we could, legally: Oxfam, Sue Ryder and in British Heart Foundation he bought, *Soledad Brother. The Prison Letters of George Jackson*. Angus waved the old Penguin paperback in my face. 'My third copy.' He also bought a *Venice* t-shirt, with sequins. 'Reduced, cause of the cold snap,' he claimed. Leaving, he'd stepped out the door first; the old blue rinse behind the till, immediately said to her male colleague, 'Isn't that long haired thing barred from here?'

Angus and I went clambering back across the ice embankments towards the canal.

'Let's play a wee game,' he smiled. I was disquieted. Angus used to challenge me to shoot at his bare arse with an airgun. Now he kneeled before the wire fence, in the snow. 'Touch the wire, with your tongue; see how long you can keep it there before it sticks.'

'No ways.'

'C'mon, chicken. Look.' His charmless tongue emerged and its tip contacted the wire. I grimaced, but after almost a minute he darted his tongue back in. I sighed and kneeled. I cannily put my tongue out and it touched the rusted wire. After only a few seconds, I tried to draw back, but my tongue resisted. It was horribly adhered to the fence wire. 'Uhhh.'

Angus cackled. There was nothing for it. I jerked my head aside and a needle of pain filled my mouth. A tiny portion of my tongue tissue remained lodged on the trembling, frozen wire.

'Plonker. You make sure there's warm saliva *over* on your tongue first.'

It started snowing before we reached his house.

'Jeez-oh,' he said. 'This rate, we'll be climbing in the first floor windows.'

It snowed lightly for two days and the deep cold just wouldn't shift. Each morning, Angus would look out at the back garden and say, 'The crust is just too hard. Get *Alien* on.' The radio reports from the ski community were ecstatic. Busiest season in their history.

I showered two times over at the garage. I'd asked Angus for shampoo, but he'd handed me the Fairy washing up liquid from beside the kitchen sink. There had been ice in my hair by the time I got back over those damned fields.

One morning we were slumped with familiar expectation before the unpleasant biological imperatives of *Alien Resurrection*. We could speak out all the dialogue before it was delivered. Our lips moving silently, obediently, to Hollywood's triumph. During a merciful pause in the pounding soundtrack, we both heard a giant subterranean event outside. At the bottom of the back garden, the huge deposit of cat litter had crashed down through the ice of the frozen canal, leaving a dark hole filled with bobbing stools; water seeped up over the ragged ice edges.

'It's begun,' Angus whispered. Then he added, 'Away back up the stair and bring over the pee bucket.'

Before midday, we had hitched from the Shell garage. Angus vaguely knew the driver of a white works van. In the cab, we all sat side by side, the road measured by long cables of brown slush, moving in under the van's high windscreen. 'That's two eagles I've seen the day,' the driver commented dryly. 'Two Eddie the Eagles. Never knew you indulged, Gus?'

It was true; we looked odd. We wore beany hats, professional climbing boots, orange waterproof waders from the fish factory and Rohan ski jackets with mountaineering gloves. I hid an ice pick under my jacket. The long ski bag was slung in the rear.

'Strictly the nursery slopes,' Angus sneered.

Where he dropped us off, the trucks made deafening, passing hisses, along the strewn road. Angus slung the long ski bag across his shoulder.

We made it halfway up the steep access road, looked each way and both suspiciously clambered into a windbreak of pines where we waited it out. Dusk was so swift, you could see the daylight die around you. It had started to snow lightly again.

In the last moments of daylight, we both leaned to the daunting ascent. Covering the gradient up under the cable car pylons was toughest. It was so steep I used the ice pick and we didn't need to see what way was upward in the unbroken darkness. We gasped higher, then lay flat and still when the last cable car of the day came down, squeaking invisibly above us. The cable car windows chucked out swift advances of yellow light, which swept down the black mountain in two blocks, on either side of the pylons, but pure darkness lay beneath, where we cowered. Then we pummelled on up. I wasn't so fit anymore and felt tears run down my cheeks. We crossed the impacted feel of a piste.

'Just a ski tow.'

It was midnight by the time we reached it.

We both lay down, breathing hard and cursing, and yet it still snowed. He started unzipping the skis bag. I strapped the whelk-picker nightlight, like a miner's lamp, onto my forehead.

Angus carefully folded the ski bag back up. 'Beautiful, isn't she?'

'Aye.'

'Pulse induction. No mineralisation interference. Fires a pulse.'

Angus squinted upward, aligning himself exactly with the chair lift wires above, though I couldn't distinguish them in the falling snow. He began sweeping from side to side as he moved up the mountainside and in about two minutes he tapped the earphones and pointed. I dove in with the ice pick.

'Canny, canny, might be fragile.'

I had to take off my gloves and my frozen fingers probed. In the beam of light, I pulled up a pair of golden sunglasses from the sparkling snow crystals.

'Ray-Bans. Polarised,' he whispered in a religious tone.

Further up we got three mobile phones, one after another, then the first wallet. Three hundred in cash. Then a TAG Heuer Carrera. We got a stupid Timex too, which I just tossed well aside.

'The hell with the Jacobite Gold. This is today's treasure. Dropped spoils of the yuppies.' Angus snarled, 'And it all pours down like silver,' as he swept the metal detector from side to side before him, moving on up ahead, beneath the chair lifts.

He used red golf tees to mark the spots where he got a signal, then carried on up the slope. I dug out at each red tee and followed almost a hundred yards behind. I threw aside the scourge of numerous ski-poles and even some Red Bull cans – one still full, but frozen like a rock – so I saved it for dawn. I placed the valuable spoils and whole wallets into a canvas bag.

Suddenly the snow stopped, then later the full moon surged free of the cloud and lit up the entire mountainside with a wave of generous and ghostly light. It was an unforgettable sight, those huge harvests of virgin snow flooded under moonlight. I could work without the torch, from golf tee to golf tee.

Around three in the morning, we'd pulled two more laden wallets, ski goggles, more Ray-Bans, an umbrella, a pocketful of change and a jiggered Blackberry. We'd cleared the second chair lift and crossed to the third. I reckon we had a grand in cash alone. Angus was calling, 'Last year, high school kids was up here to scavenge, but only after the snow melted. Beat them all to it. You got to use the available technology.'

We swapped. I used the metal detector and planted the tees. Just into that third chair lift, I saw Angus had fallen very far behind. I unstrapped the metal detector and turned sideways, came slowly back down. He was kneeling by a huge excavation with the ice pick sunk in extracted snow.

Angus said, in a neutral tone, 'Aye. Must've come straight down into three foot of soft stuff.'

I looked over the edge in the moonlight.

'Billy Nae Mates. No a peep on the radio. What's society coming to?'

The man lay face up, eyes closed, black cheeks en-smeared with frost, glistening in the moon glow. One of his ski poles had bent sideways. What sickened me, was that Angus had forced back the guy's frozen jacket and looted him for cash only, then replaced the wallet and identification. Didn't touch the credit cards. He had forced off the wrist watch as well, and broken the strap. He was daintily picking up the individual links from the snow. Angus looked upward at me and shook his head disappointedly. 'This'll all melt in a few days and they'll get him. Nothing to do with us.'

We re-entombed the poor man, stamping down the snow upon his grave. Yet even I admitted, we couldn't help him. So we tramped on up, with our long and clear blue shadows. Magpie-ing out the loot from that shining mountainside, lifting our trophies to the moon as the world cracked and tinkled, agitatedly and judging, all around us in that milk night.

# NINETY-NINE TAE WAN AGAINST

## Jane Alexander

Twenty teenagers, an hour from freedom. Carla could feel it: the stifled energy shimmering over bent heads, the hot breeze of whispers rippling through the classroom.

She put down her stylo – *click* – and gave them her basilisk stare. They were a good lot, this class, most of the time. But, Friday afternoon ... Besides which, they were unsettled. They knew she was leaving.

When the whispers had subsided, she lifted her stylo again. On Monday, Rosalie Simpson would take over. Everything had to be ready: essay questions, marking schemes. Outside the window, the sky was pink and distant, fat clouds blooming on the horizon. She shifted in her seat, felt it re-form around her altered shape. She'd be here all evening, if she didn't focus.

*What were the values that informed the introduction of the Open Door Policy?*

She was sorry not to be teaching this module. It always grabbed their enthusiasm. They could see the subject in themselves, their families and friends; it held the same solipsistic appeal as those personality quizzes that so fascinated the girls. And for her it was satisfying – watching them turn their considerable energies towards their own recent history.

In a corner of the classroom, laughter bubbled up. Gerry. It always seemed to be Gerry – unless she just noticed him more. It was his misfortune: one light head in a field of brown and black. Mind, even Gerry seemed to be darkening, tone by tone, term by term. You wouldn't call him fair, not any more. Mouse, you'd have to say.

With an effort, Carla got to her feet. Twenty teenagers raised wary eyes.

'*I* don't want to stay behind,' she announced. Instantly, their eyes dropped to their screens. 'But obviously *you* do...'

Really, she wasn't that sorry to be going.

Focus...

*Describe the period of decline that preceded the introduction of the Open Door Policy.*

> *Economic crash: ___ / 10*
> *Oil crisis:___ / 10*
> *Second Depression: ___ / 10*
> *Mass emigration: ___ / 10*
> *Score: ___ / 40*

Additional marks awarded for correct use of statistics. Population decline: fifty percent, between 2015 and 2025. Lowest recorded population density: thirty people per kilometre. Gran had remembered it, had grown up through it, in a different Scotland. We were dying, she'd said. Simple as that. We had nothing but empty space.

*Analyse the key factors that led to the successful integration of New Scots following the introduction of the Open Door Policy.*

Gran's parents had been mentors, among the first: paired with a family newly arrived from China. The daughter, Jackie, still lived in Perth: for fifty years she'd sent Gran cards at Christmas. Once Gran had gone, she'd addressed them to Carla's dad – *Donald, and family.* Now they came to *Carla, and family.*

So long as they could work, Carla's gran had said, we were happy enough tae see them. Cos we needed them, didn't we? Wherever it was they'd come fae. And then when we saw our country coming back tae life ... Workers for the clean industries; shops opening, new businesses. Bairns. So many bairns. There were some against it still – so much had changed, you see, so fast – but no many. No many.

*Outline some additional consequences of the Open Door Policy.*

Och, you wouldn't believe what we ate, her gran used to say. She'd been fond of disgusting her granddaughter with descriptions of macaroni cheese encased in hot-water pastry, of pizza slicked with batter and deep-fried. Best forgotten, Gran had said. Then there was all the songs no-one remembers now. *Oh ye cannae fling a piece oot a twenty-storey flat ...* And we used to tease your dad about how rare he was, how he was on the road tae extinction. We did, we laughed about that.

At some point, Carla supposed, people must have stopped laughing.

She looked out over her classroom, a dark head at each desk. Earlier this year she'd been working with Graeme Kwan on a cross-curricular research project: life science and social history. Graeme's department had picked up a dozen old DNA scanners. The idea was for S4 students to scan each other: to trace the incidence of the MC1R recessive variant gene, and compare their results to Scotland's population of a hundred years ago.

What would be really interesting, Graeme had said, would be a partnership project, with somewhere like Newhope High. But, politically ...

Politically – yes. She'd seen the difficulty. If integration was something to be proud of, its opposite, logically, was an embarrassment. In the outskirts, those low-rise housing belts around the biotech facilities, the recycling centres, the decontam plants – the places where new and indigenous Scots had mixed the least – you still saw evidence of MC1R mutation. At inter-school tournaments, when a busload of kids arrived from Newhope, occasionally you saw them: those pale redheads. And they did seem paler than redheads used to be. Perhaps it was the colour capture of the recent past: how the old digital media were so easily manipulated, and people back then so dissatisfied with reality – turning the colours up a fraction, up a fraction more, to make their lives that little bit brighter. Sky bluer, grass greener. Redheads redder. Whatever the reason, the kids from the belts looked spiritless, bleached: faded hair floating round dinner-plate faces. Nothing like Carla's dad, in his prime. The way she liked to remember him. Soaring above her, sun at his back, blurred bright across her vision.

The project would still go ahead, if Rosalie was keen.

Outside, a fresh leaf-fall swirled past the window, a flash of autumn colour. Copper. Rust. Red.

Come to think of it, had there been a card last Christmas? A card from Jackie? Carla couldn't remember, now. It didn't matter – only, that's how you found out. That's how you knew another connection with the past had frayed to nothing.

It was her fraying past that had caused the trouble, last year. She had spoiled Christmas by insisting everything had to be just the same. The same as what? her husband had asked. The same as it *used* to be ... The girls had wanted animated decorations: she'd insisted on the old cool-flame candles. Dev's mum had brought starters for Christmas lunch, hot fresh pakora, and Carla had picked at hers with bad grace. When Dev had refused Christmas pudding in favour of fruit, she'd had to leave the table. He'd followed her into the kitchen. Tell me, he'd said. But it was two years since dad had died, in the dip between Christmas and Hogmanay, and she shouldn't be sad anymore: not this sharp-toothed grief that still bit deep. She was being unreasonable, and she knew it.

On the 31st she'd made an effort to see the new year in – make-up, perfume, silky dress. The girls had been allowed to stay up for the fireworks – streamed in 4D, the smell of frost and gunpowder right in their living room. Dev had pretended to enjoy a whisky with her, a nod to tradition. And at half past twelve, when the girls had been packed off to sleep, he had turned in too.

Alone, Carla had poured several inches of whisky. Breathed the vapour from her glass, and conjured the parties her folks had thrown when she was a girl. Laughing, dancing, singing – kisses and cheers at the bells – and drink, and drink, her ten-year-old self giddy on the fumes. She wallowed, till she felt familiar misery knocking on her chest, and then she jumped to her feet. Drained her glass, grabbed the bottle, and stepped out into the snow.

First-footing. It was something her pupils heard of in cultural identity class; something even her parents had stories of rather than memories. It was nothing people did. But that night strangers invited her in, and she drank with them till the whisky dissolved the weight in her chest. She drank till the night fragmented; she drank, and at some point she turned her head and caught an astonishing sight. The sun at midnight, in midwinter.

What happened next was something to do with the urge towards light. To do with the fire of the whisky.

Waking to low morning light that pooled in the sheet-white scoop of his back, that made a beacon of his head on the pillow next to hers. Realising everything was in danger, and that she felt quite safe. Reaching out: easing her fingers into the flames of his hair.

The heat of her, on the short walk home – guilt and lust – should have melted the snow.

That evening she'd hauled herself from her bed just as the kids were heading for theirs. Drunk a litre of water, eaten dry toast. Apologised to her husband. It's alright, he'd said, not like you do it all the time. Tradition, isn't it. He'd stroked her cheek, gently, and murmured: Feeling better...?

By the end of January the snow was a memory. The year was opening up: a slow crack of the door. And Carla was certain, of one thing at least.

*Imaginative Response: if the Open Door Policy had not been introduced, what might Scotland be like today?*

Some pupils struggled with Imaginative Response. She had to lead them through it, ask them: what if...? Suggest they think of the countries where borders had been closed: of England, or the Formerly United States. Or look at Iceland, whose citizens could trace their families back to about ten ancestors, and probably forward to as few descendants: homogenous and doomed. The brighter kids ran wild with I.R., had twenty-second century Scots on the brink of extinction, surviving on oats and kale. Last year one boy had invented *ScotWorld!* – the entire nation transformed into a themepark, kept afloat on tourist yuan. What if you could run with gangs in Glasgow; catch guga off Lewis; watch the Northern Lights nightly? He'd got top marks for that.

What if. More than anything, that's what history was for her. The streams of possibility, where it could have gone differently: splitting off from what actually happened; instantly evaporating. Leaving only a faint trace of *what if?*

The light dimmed a fraction. Carla glanced up, as the spectrum shifted from blue towards pink. From study to relaxation: the end of the school day. The kids sat blinking, eager to be dismissed.

'Okay, finish off what you're working on – remember to palm out ... Before you go – as you know, Ms Simpson will be teaching you from next week. She'll prepare you for your exams, in which I'm sure you will all do very well. Does anyone have any questions? Yes: Alina.'

Alina lowered her hand, flicked back an over-long fringe. 'Have you decided on a name?'

'Questions about this class.'

'I know, but have you?'

'We've thought of a few.' It was a diverse list she and Dev had come up with: Indian, for his side of the family; Cuban, for her mother's side. Scottish, for her dad's. 'It depends, obviously, what sort it is.'

Behind her fringe, Alina looked blank.

Carla sighed. 'Girl or boy.'

Girl or boy. For a boy, she liked Angus: her dad's middle name. Still. They would have to wait and see.

Five o'clock, and finally everything was fit to be left. Carla palmed out of the network, hauled herself from her chair. She paused for a last look round the classroom: its desks vacant, its screens powered down.

'Lights,' she said, and the room sank into darkness.

There was a new display in the corridor: S3, human geography. It sprang to life as she passed. Pulsing lines on a world map traced the journeys made by New Scots from south, east and west, all arrows pointing to Scotland. Her gaze lit on Cuba, and up popped the names and faces of all the S3 pupils with Cuban ancestry. The Cuban Scots dimmed as she looked towards India, were replaced by a dozen third years with Indian heritage.

'Impressive, eh?' Graeme Kwan was standing beside her.

'Very.' It reminded her of those ancient book illustrations of where people had come from: Africa, the cradle of humankind. The long movement, immensely slow, to where they stood now. To light skin, light eyes, lightened hair. It struck her that the same thing would happen again. That in tens of thousands of years – when the fresh faces on the display had been gone an unimaginable length of time – the north would once more have its way.

'Finishing up today?' Graeme asked. 'Not before time, it looks like...'

She smiled. 'On the home stretch now. Hey, Graeme –' She shouldn't ask. She knew she shouldn't ask. But she'd tried to work it out, and the probabilities were beyond her. She needed to hear it from someone she could trust to know. 'Remember the project we worked on? MC1R?'

'I do. It's going ahead, you know. Rosalie's agreed.'

'Oh, great; that's great. Well, I was wondering –' she patted her bump – 'do you think, would it be possible for this one to have red hair? Just because, my father did. My father was properly red.'

Graeme was smiling, shaking his head. 'I wouldn't have said it's likely.'

'But in theory. I mean, I'm dark, and obviously Dev is dark. The girls are both dark. But – that doesn't mean it's impossible?'

'No, not impossible. Just hugely unlikely. It's complicated, the genetics of red hair. More complicated, the more we know about it. Even if we knew you were a carrier – and presuming Dev isn't – I still couldn't give you odds. But, stab in the dark?'

Carla nodded.

'Less than one in a hundred.'

'Right.' Not impossible. Just *ninety-nine tae wan* against. 'And if Dev did have red hair...?'

'Much more likely, obviously. What, are you wanting a redhead?'

*Yes – no – yes –* 'I hadn't thought: for some reason it just struck me –'

'I could probably work it out – but it'd take me so long, you'll find out sooner than me!'

Two weeks. Nowhere near soon enough.

Every day, the metro took her past his turning. She didn't know, today, that she was going to get off – not till she'd requested the stop. Didn't know she would count the steps back to his road, would stand looking down the terraced row that split off from the main street.

She'd never seen him, since. She could almost convince herself she'd imagined the whole thing.

Windows were lighting up, promising warmth. She wasn't sure if she saw a light at his window – couldn't, in fact, be sure which house was his. She tugged her coat round her, stretching it over her belly where it didn't quite meet. Watched the sun sink below the rooftops, catching on rags of cloud. A vanishing flare of orange and red.

Angus: or, for a girl, she liked Ailsa.

It would be dark soon: the year was turning again. She shivered. Pointed herself towards home. Started to walk.

# THE VILLAGE

## Tom Pow


We were evacuated at the end;
each of our roads simply a sea
     no one cared to cross. For what

did we want to stay? they asked–
in a place no more than a sum
     of boarded up buildings;

a cemetery too loquacious,
too full. We told them we lived
     within the idea of the village–

its silent school, its songless church,
its shop with nothing to sell. Still,
     memory kept a full roll, dipped

a head in prayer, lingered at the shop–
though with *better things to do*–
     for the chance of a bit of gossip.

The village had been stripped of all ages,
but our own. We stood on its prow,
     waiting for it to take us down.

\*\*\*


Yet here I am in this new building.
Well-lit and warm, I think of a cattle shed;
     us all safe in our stalls. So where

are you from? they ask. The name
crumbles on my tongue. Their accents
      are all foreign. Where are *they* from?

I forget. They smile, as they help me
to my feet and lead me from place
      to place. They dab food from my chin.

You're from Scotland, they tell me.
*Scotland.* Ah, yes. I'll nod all day,
      if it helps me to stay close to kindness.

# INTO THE GARDEN

## Alice Walsh

Callum waited for the sound of the doctor's car driving off before he could bear to look again at his mother's face. Jean's hand twitched. Loosely clasped in his, the signal was meaningless as it was not in her control. She had lost the use of her hands some time ago as the disease closed down her motor functions. The illness became apparent seven years ago. Her intelligence and awareness had not been affected, that was not a part of it. But enough of all that, she was tired now, sick to the teeth dealing with it, thinking about it, talking about it. They all were. Her decision was made, the drug was now in place. Callum would activate it when she was ready, when she indicated that it was time.

'Call me later,' the doctor had said as Callum saw him to the door, his manner pleasant, professional, involved yet not intrusive. He knew Jean very well and had attended to Callum too as a boy, made light of his broken collar-bone when he had fallen from a tree aged thirteen, and told his mother to feed him nothing but the best ice-cream when he was nine and it was murder to swallow.

Jean was propped in her chair, her head leaned over to her right, a tissue beneath her chin to catch errant saliva. Her concentration was fully focused onto Callum's face, as though learning him off by heart. He tried to bear this steadily, and found it too hard. He did not feel strong. Again it would be about him, taking away from the enormity of her leaving life. Ach, shut up, they had been through all this, were becoming bored of it, in truth.

He held her gaze for some seconds longer before checking his phone to see if Catherine had left a message. She was meant to be here before now.

It was 19 April 2019, Good Friday as it happened. The airwaves were awash with Requiems and stories of the Passion. The churches had raised huge wooden crosses at various points across the town for the people to follow the Stations of the Cross and partake of the agonies of the first century AD. It had been a fringe activity when it started more than a decade ago. Now the event was massive and grew more elaborate with every year. Callum thought it was part of a need for older certainties after the economic meltdown which was still playing out, a fear of the future combined with a breakdown of trust in government and scientific reason. Callum was a medical doctor and he knew it would be busy at the hospital today. Last year he had treated a man who had worn barbed wire under his shirt for the duration of Lent, to express solidarity, he said, for interned prisoners across the world. The man was not even a Christian. Nevertheless he had leapt forward to help carry the cross, got caught in the crush, and was taken to Accident and Emergency along with twenty-five others. Although this man was undoubtedly ill, he was not an immediate danger to himself or to others and was sent on his way with his wounds cleanly dressed and a handful of penicillin.

Though his mind was occupied with private grief Callum sensed unhingement in the air. A minority of vocal people had eagerly taken to the hair shirt, abandoning consumerism and embracing fundamentalism of various strands. Others, less flagrantly than before, enjoyed the good life as long as they had the means. Most people just got by with less and tried to make some sort of future for their families. The police were always alert for trouble. There were usually eruptions wherever crowds gathered.

Callum suspected his mother of irony, choosing this particular day to end her suffering, though she had always said that when she could no longer swallow, that would be her limit. They had already delayed this moment and it was unfair to prolong it. At least, he thought, they would not have to watch as she starved herself to death, thanks to the End of Life Assistance Act passed three years ago by the Scottish Parliament in an unusually strong stand by politicians across party lines holding their position in the face of religious opposition. Jean had been a staunch supporter of that bill and had used her organisational skills to good effect to generate support for it. Callum too had been enlisted to the cause, rather against his inclination at first until his experiences as a medical student confirmed his resolution. He glanced at his phone again. What was keeping Catherine, today of all days?

In the bedroom the orthopaedic bed hissed and sighed rhythmically. He walked through to unplug it, it would not be needed again. Jean was beyond speech, though her hearing was still good. He read aloud to her Catherine's message. She would be here soon. Her usual route was closed for the procession. The High Street had temporarily become the Via Dolorosa. He supposed the knoll at Craigie would stand once again for the Hill of Calvary. There was keen competition for the role of Jesus.

One of his colleagues at the hospital would this year play Pilate. The pageant had gone global. It was broadcast live on the net by all the major evangelist channels. It was the biggest event of the year for this tourism dependent town, supported by the town council, sponsored by local businesses and grossing millions.

Callum remembered more joyful Easters in the past.

'I'm thinking about that time you took us all camping, it was twenty years ago this week you know.'

Jean's face contorted into what he knew was a smile. She remembered it well, the two highly excited boys, Callum and his pal Jonny, nine years old and ready for anything. Catherine had come too with a friend. Jean had been surprised that they were up for it, those sophisticated teenagers. She drove out west beyond Lochearnhead looking for a good camping place near to water and not too far from the road. She tried several places along Strathearn and Glen Ogle, dismayed by the quantities of broken glass and other rubbish strewn around. She kept driving west until she found the place where they had once stopped for a picnic, away from the main road beyond Tyndrum. They had been driven mad by the midges that July, but it was too early for them in April. It was a good place to camp, far enough from the main road and with no forbidding signs tacked about. There was a flat grassy space for their tents and someone had made a ring of rocks by the burn for the fire. The boys put their tent up in five minutes, and were gathering wood, competing with each other for the biggest sticks. The girls struggled with their tent, an ancient one belonging to Catherine's friend. Jean tried to help them but for the life of her could not see how it worked. They would all have to share together. They carried bedding from the car, inflated mattresses, tried out the torches until she told them to save the batteries, and opened the packets of crisps meant to stave off panic if the food took too long. They cooked chicken pieces and sausages on a mesh over the fire, heated noodles in a pan and made toast. She remembered that she burned the meat to make sure it was cooked through. Darkness fell early in their elevated valley and the temperature quickly dropped below freezing once the sun sank behind the mountain. They shivered and bunched up close to the fire, clutching their cups of hot chocolate, gazing at the stars, millions of them and no moon to steal away their shine. Catherine went away for a pee only to wet her pants when a silent sheep uttered a loud baa directly behind her. They laughed about that for years. Jean remembered her anxiety as a car pulled up nearby, the engine running. What would she do, just herself and four children? Why did she do this without another adult? She remembered the relief as the car pulled away, and her watchfulness afterwards. When the Tornadoes roared up the valley on night manoeuvres she vented her anxiety by raging at the skies, though they were finished in half an hour. The boys loved the planes and asked endless questions about the sky. She pointed to Orion glittering magnificently, and to the Plough which Callum said looked like a question mark. The girls grew tired of nature and shared pictures on their phones, regretting the lack of coverage for texting friends back east. Jean watched for shooting stars until the cold forced her to zip the tent flap shut.

Next morning was clear and bright. She got the fire started, the kettle boiling, the embers just right for toast and rashers. The girls, finding no alternative, decided to wash in the river. The boys were ahead of them, plunging into the freezing water, egging each other on and shrieking about their shrivelled willies. Oh, those blues and greens were never so vivid. She felt so good to have got them to this place, to be enjoying this with them.

Callum remembered that they explored the bank of the river that their burn joined as it rushed west to the sea. The water level was low, it had been a dry spring. The river was full of rocks, smooth and rounded, like Henry Moore sculptures, Jean had said. One huge boulder had a hole right the way through it, at least a metre deep. Callum climbed into it and it reached up to his neck. There was a photo of that and one of Jonny too, making ghoulish faces as if they were beheaded. He remembered the leathery flattened frog on the narrow road, at the other side of the belt of forestry. Mum had called them across to see it, for educational reasons. The next day they went back to the same place, only this time he and Jonny forced their way through the forestry for the fun of it. They came across a tent in a small clearing and called to Jean, who was on the riverbank nearby. The girls were back at base making soup with the remains of the food. Jean told the boys to come away and they obeyed her. There was a bad smell and the tent was torn and green with mildew. She caught up with them a few minutes later. She said they must pack up now and go home, and although they were loudly disappointed, and hadn't eaten the soup yet, she insisted.

Callum never knew that the tent contained the remains of a young man, an artist from the south of England who had gone missing the previous winter. He had come far north, maybe to get a break from his troubles, but they had come with him. The cold spring and the dense forestry had preserved his anonymity.

Jean had been transfixed by his partly eaten face, the jaws apart, the teeth white and even. Her immediate thought was that he had been murdered and she was gripped with terror that it might have been hers that were taken, last night even. Her overriding urge was to escape from this place. Afterward, she learned that the man, just a boy really, was deeply loved by his family and friends. He had a history of depression and had apparently overdosed, alone. The family were grateful to know at last what had happened. She read an article in a newspaper about him several months later, written by his sister who seemed to understand and accept his choice. Jean always wondered whether his parents ever had.

As Jean was lost in these old memories, Catherine arrived on her bicycle, out of breath and sweating. She had come by the outer ring road though it added five miles to her journey across town from the convent. Callum went to meet her and she embraced him rather stiffly, called a greeting to her mother, and went upstairs to her old room.

She changed out of her grey skirt and jumper into a green silk dress, an old one her mother had always loved to see her wear. Around her neck was the pearl necklace that had belonged to their grandmother. Once he saw her come back downstairs Callum felt profoundly relieved. The day had warmed up and they moved to the garden, Callum wheeled Jean's chair into place and Catherine carried the tea-tray to the little table under the cherry blossom, such startling white against the blue of the sky, when you looked up. They sat for some time, one on each side of Jean on their wrought iron chairs, saying little.

An hour passed and Catherine rose from where she knelt beside her mother, the still hands entwined now with a set of rosary beads. The Act of Contrition had been spoken into the dead woman's ear. They sat awhile each lost in silence, before Callum moved slowly inside to make a few phone calls.

# THE FÀILTE POLICY

## Raman Mundair

Just like Nuestra Señora de la Candelaria, the Canarians had said when they found her near dead on the beach.

They'd said that she rose from the sea riding on the crest of a wave, her hands cupping her pregnant belly. Her wet skin shimmering with a coating of black sand. She gleamed a holy iridescence.

She accepted their kindness and she accepted 'Morenita' as her name.

By the time the bus had reached the town centre she knew that the driver's name was Les. He had an open, friendly face and everyone getting on the bus seemed to know his name. The bus drew up at the Bridge Street stop where people were waiting. First in line was a large, middle-aged red-faced man carrying a stuffed black bin liner. As the door of the bus opened the driver jokingly called to him.

'Oh naw, Dod! Y'cannae take that on the bus.'

The big man immediately responded, 'C'mon, Les, Ah've got tae take it on. That's Julie! I punctured her last night!'

The two men laughed and people smiled. She looked closely at the bag as the man went by. She could see a patch of quilt through a tear in the bag. She felt her disquiet melt away and laughed at herself as she looked out of the window at the grey granite of the street. She reminded herself that she was now in a place where bodies weren't found hidden or abandoned in bags as a matter of course.

Her head covered in plastic and held under water, she wanted her last breath to be her unborn child's name. She exhaled his name.

Later, on her knees in the dark, her hands strapped behind her back she thought about the child. Had he known he was so close to death? He kicked her ribs in answer.

The bus jolted sharply at the red light. She lurched forward and caught the handrail to steady herself. The big red faced-man bantered with the driver.

'Hey Les, ye've got an awfa heavy fit the day, man!'

'You be quiet, Dod Smith, or Ah'll pit ye aff the bus!'

'Eh? Ah know mah rights. Nae doot Ah'll be puttin in a complaint aboot you.'

'Go on. Hit 'im! Hit 'im!' a couple of old ladies chimed in.

Laughter rippled through the bus. She found herself smiling with the other passengers.

The child had forced the decision. Once the child became an inevitability they knew they couldn't tread water forever.

How could they raise the child in a land that tortured their bodies and silenced their voices? How could they let them claim the child as one of their own, stain him with the corrupt and the poisoned? How could they teach him to live furtive dreams? How could they let the child grow and see his parents mime an existence that he would believe was life?

A tall, young man got on the bus with a cat-sized dog on a lead. They made a strangely well suited couple. The creature yapped and nipped at shoes and ankles as its owner made his way up the aisle. She looked at the man's face. Something about his eyes, nose, hair and gait gave him an appearance more canine than human. He sat down on the seat in front of her and opened a parcel of fish and chips. A strong aroma of fried food and vinegar enveloped her. She watched the man eat and noticed him stoop forward and feed each alternate chip to his drooling dog.

'A nation's true heart is reflected in its hospitality,' her Grandfather used to enjoy saying – usually as he opened up a bottle of black market whisky to toast visiting scholars she had brought back from the university to offer them a taste of 'traditional life'. She couldn't show the visitors the naked truth so she would show them her people's creativity – the ways they tried to make their lives significant and beautiful with small, strong things like laughter, food, friendship, poetry and music.

With the betrayal everything that had nourished her died: the sound of her language, music, poetry – the taste of her people's food.

She wanted nothing to do with it now. It was too painful.

In the seat across from her two children in school uniforms were shar-ing a packet of sweeties. Random sweets that didn't appear to meet their expectations were rejected and dropped carelessly onto the floor.

In Scotland she couldn't get enough of sugar. She wanted sweetness in her mouth. Shortbread, macaroons, chocolate, ice cream, doughnuts – anything to displace the taste of salt and the smell of the sea from the crossing that continued to revisit her in nightmares.

A woman with a baby in a buggy and an array of bags struggled onto the bus. Dog-man stood and gave up his seat and the woman gratefully sat down. The baby was swaddled in bright cartoon colours, its face barely visible. The bus rattled and shook as it crossed over the cobbled bridge. The baby awoke and began to wail. The dog barked sharply and snapped at the buggy wheels.

She turned her head and looked down-river, beyond the harbour, towards the sea.

The sea.

He had been a strong swimmer. When they had met at college he was on the diving team. She had loved to watch him. The impossible fall, head down, his arms slicing through the water; his shoulder muscles when he climbed out of the pool; the way the water glistened and clung to his body; his smile when she called him 'Dolphin Boy'.

In the storm light he had grabbed part of the wreckage as the waves continued to smash over them. He used his belt to fasten her to it to keep her afloat. He held onto the other end, the waves lashing their bodies. He looked into her eyes and told her everything would be okay, that the three of them would be free and safe soon. He kept eye contact until at last, exhausted, she fell asleep.

The bus speeded up. A handful of gulls moiled up into the sky and were caught wheeling in the pale light over the harbour. She closed her eyes and looked away.

She had awoken to the sound of gulls and a sea dappled brilliant with sun diamonds. It took her a moment to realise that he was gone.

She was filled with the terror of seeing the ocean surrounding her as far as she could see.

The bus sighed to a halt and nearly emptied. A few people got on. There were plenty of seats but the old woman came and settled beside her. They smiled briefly at one another. The woman looked frail, dressed in flimsy clothes: light layers with an old, heavy, oversized man's coat. She glanced down at the woman's hands – the dry, transparent, blue-veined skin. The delicate fingers were cradling a small pineapple. The woman caught her looking.

'It's my wee bit of sunshine,' she explained. 'Everybody needs a taste of sunshine in the winter, eh? It keeps yer spirits up.'

In Tenerife she had been out in the sun all day selling cheap jewellery in the street. She had seen hundreds of pale bodies visit the island to worship the sun.

In the place they had run from the sun was constant. The sun set the rhythm of the day. It beat time for work, for rest. It dictated the harvest of the land and flavoured the food. She had loved the quality of light and the way it softened reality. She had been a heliotrope – turning her face towards the sun to let the bright light blind her; let the heat leave her woozy and stunned, too tired to have to think.

The old woman glanced out of the window and announced, 'Rain on the way. If ye've got any washin' oot you best bring it in. Ah'm away home tae get mine.' She cupped the pineapple up to her nose and sniffed.

She hated intense bright heat now. She appreciated the comfort of intermittent Scottish summers and enjoyed the rain when it came, letting it cleanse her, letting the wind blow through the empty hollow inside her. She hated the memory of the warmth of the sun and the true blue of the sea. She preferred the pale northern skies and seas. She welcomed the cold – the way it brought her mind back to the present and not suspended in some dank, fruitless gully of the past.

He would have fought for life.
They both knew what it felt like to drown.

A harsh wind came off the sea and snaked inside as the old woman and her pineapple left the bus. She felt it lick her cheek. She shivered and pulled her coat closer. She looked down at the empty space beside her and felt an absence.

The letter had arrived in the morning. Her appeal had failed. Someone had decided that she wasn't eligible to stay and that she now had fourteen days in which to leave. She stayed drowning in the harsh light of her room until late afternoon. Finally she put the child in a sling and went down to the beach to hawk jewellery to the holidaymakers. She wandered aimlessly and sold nothing.

Her head began to throb. She felt nauseous, weak, short of breath. It was a dry, airless day and the iron-hot fingers of the sun jabbed her towards the shoreline. She put her feet into the cool water and allowed the sea to come to her again. The waves drew in and pulled and tugged against her legs, the coarse, dark sand falling away beneath her feet. She felt herself sinking.

She was ready to surrender when the baby awoke and moved restlessly.

It was then that she first heard of the Fàilte Policy.

The driver had been whistling a vaguely familiar tune when he stopped short and called out to his friend.

'Eh, Dod! Mind yer stop.'

The red faced man got to his feet.

'Cheers Les! See ye tomorra!'

'Aye, see ye tomorra.'

The big man waved as he stepped off the bus. The driver began to pull away but immediately came to a juddering stop. The doors swung open.

'Forget somethin', did ye?' the driver laughed.

Dod got back on and retrieved his black bin bag.

'Thanks, Les. Ah'll fergit me heed wan o these days.'

'See ya later, man.'

Dod and 'Julie' left the bus. The driver turned the corner at the library and her stop came into view.

She had spread her cloth on the sea wall and laid out the pieces of jewellery. Her head still ached and she felt drained, exhausted. The sun beat down. She was sitting feeding the child when a young tourist couple stopped beside her to take a look at the jewellery.

They were from Scotland and chatted with her awhile, the young woman cooing at the baby and finally asking if she could hold him. They asked and she told them where she had come from. They bought a few pieces and had walked away when they suddenly turned back. They told her about the 'Fàilte Policy' – about how Scotland had decided that when she finally became independent in the new year she would open her borders and allow all who needed sanctuary to come and take refuge. The man scribbled down some information and pressed the paper into her palm and wished her luck.

She thanked the driver and stepped off the bus at the stop near the nursery. She paused a moment before going in to pick up her son. The low afternoon sun grazed her face. She tilted her head back to catch the dying rays. A swirling flock of starlings looped and spun across the sky. She watched the fluid folding and unfolding movements of the birds. She breathed deeply and let a lightness fall into her step.

# WITH A BIT OF LUCK

## Michael Rigg

*Poetry is language with a little luck in it*
William Stafford

There'll come a day when poets rule the land
all laws repealed and brand new words soon found
to sing our country's wonders to the world.
An hourly verse will mark the end of time
each morning's task completed with a rhyme
as sentences are measured for their sound
not sense. The stuffy schools will close, books hurled
into two piles: poetry and prose.

No doubt there'll be, as ever, some of those
stiff pedants who insist each line must scan
and half rhymes are a cheat; yet to a man
(and woman) makars will defend their right
to break the rules in every way they can
on that bright day when poets lead our land.

# LUVVABLE 'LEX IN "DRY 'N' HIGH!"

## THE WESTER HAILES WANK! (BY ROB MILLER)

### MAKE HAY WHILE THE SUN SHINES.... OAN LEITH!

AW, HULLO, READERS, HOO'S IT GAUN'? HULLO? CAN YOUSE HEAR US A'RIGHT O'ER THON BIG DIN, AY?

SEE, THON KERFUFFLE'S THE SOOND O' A WAVE O' CHANGE, KEN, SETTIN' ABOOT WASHIN' O'ER BONNY SCOTLAND THE NOO...(CHORTLE!)

WEEL, NO' FUR US A' - THE EFFECTS UR GRADUAL, KEN, EVEN IN THIS MAGIC AGE O' STUFF LIKE INSTANT MESSAGIN', INSTANT CREDIT AN' MA FAVOURITE - INSTANT SOUP (HOHO!)

BIG JESSIE'S SOUP FUR MUGS COCK-A-LEAKY FLAVOUR

HERE, IF YEEZ HUVNAE READ A' ABOOT IT IN THE PAPERS, THEN ALLOW ME.....THIS IS PURE BOILIN' HOT AFF THE PRESS, MIND...(HONK!)

CONVULSE CIDER 6.66%

LET'S SEE NOO...

SPORT GERS CHASE COAL ACE! SCOTTISH DAILY VACUUM HOOPS EYE TOP STRIKER!

HERE WE UR...JUST THERE, UNNER THE WAN ABOOT THE SCOATISH EXECUTIVE RAISIN' THE AGE LIMIT FUR BUYIN' BOOZE TAE 40! (TITTER!)

SHOCK CELEB CASH BOOZE LIMIT HITS TO! WAVE OF CHANGE SET TO BYPASS WESTER HAILES SEX! SPORT TERROR!

AYE, JUST AS AH EXPECTED - AH KIN RELAX, NAE WAVE SET TAE COME WITHIN AN INCH O'US HERE...

AH'VE SURVIVED MANY A WAVE MASEL', SO AN' AH HUV - FAE THE STOATIR IN '83, TAE THE RIPPLE O' '89, THEN '94, AN' THE BIG WAN O' '99.... AN' NO' FORGETTIN' '03 OR THE WASHOOT O' '07 AN' A'....(HOOT!)

MIND, WIR NO' A' SO LUCKY - AULD PHIL, DEID FAE THE DRINK IN '94.... AH MISSED HIS LIGHTS GAUN' OOT BY HAUF AN 'OOR.... KEN, MA AIN BATTERIES WUR PRETTY FLAT AN' A' - AH HUD A HONKIN' HANGO'ER MASEL!

AN' POOR WULLIE, MADE IT THRU THE GREAT WAVE O' '99 ONLY TAE SNUFF IT FAE AN O'ERDOSE JUST EFTER.... AH WEEL, THAT'S THE MILLENIUM DRUG FUR YE...(HAHA!)

DAFT GEORGE MADE IT, BUT, PUNTED O'ER TAE SIGHTHILL FUR EMERGENCY RE-HOOSIN' - SO HE'LL BE A'RIGHT IN FUTURE TAE.... WEEL, ASSUMIN' HIS PAST DOESNAE CATCH UP WI' HIM...

FOOL-O-BEANZ

HAUD UP! AH 'HINK THAT'S MA BOY SKULKIN' ABOOT....

HAW, DAVIE! GAUNY POP IN HERE A SEC SO'S AH KIN HUV A WORD WI' YE?(YUK!)

ASIDE FAE BURST PIPIN', RISIN' DAMP AN' YOU PISSIN' YERSEL' WHEN YIR STEAMIN' - AH DOOT THERE'S ONY CHANCE FOREIGN MOISTURE'LL FIND A WAY TAE GRACE THESE SCABBY FLOORBOARDS.

IN THE GRAND SCHEME O' THINGS THIS SCHEME IS JUST WAN O' DOZENS O' WASHED UP DODS O' POLYSTYRENE - PACKAGIN' FUR A' THE WASHED UP HUMAN FLOTSAM, ADRIFT FAE 'NORMAL' SOCIETY....

LYIN' LOW LIVES - FAE SAFT DRUGS TAE HARD KNOCKS, SMART MOOTHS TAE CASUAL SEX, REDTOPS TAE BLONDE AMBITIONS, WEE DRINKS TAE MASSIVE HANGO'ERS, BIG DEALS TAE PETTY SQUABBLES - THE UPHILL STRUGGLE O' THE DOONWARD SPIRAL.

YIR MAROONED HERE, LIKELY 'HIGH' IF NO' ENTIRELY 'DRY'...YE DINNAE BELONG BUT - AN' THIS IS WHAUR AH COME IN- WI' MA HELP YIR TIME HERE WILLNAE BE LONG...

WHO'S GOT?

ACTUALLY, PAL, AH'D RATHER YE DIDNAE COME IN, KEN....FACT IS, AH THINK YE'D BEST BE HEADIN'....

'BEHEADIN'...AYE, AH LIKE THAT....

PHH! ASK A STUPIT QUESTION, AY FOLKS? THAT'S ME TELT.... NOO, AH'VE AN 'OOR AFORE THE WIFE'S BACK FAE THE TOON- D'YEEZ FANCY JOININ' US FUR MA AIN 'INSTANT' WAVE O' CHANGE, 3 LITRES O' CIDER? (HOOT!)

THE END!

# EPIPHANY

## Allan Massie

'They set out to make a fool of me,' the old man said. 'I'm afraid they succeeded. Bastards.'

The old man was bitter. He had been bitter for a long time, with short intervals. Decades ago he had been hailed as the new star of Scottish writing. His first two novels had made him what was not yet called 'a celebrity'. 'Adam Carnie is the first truly modernist Scottish novelist,' declared the reviewer of *The Glasgow Herald*. In London too the critics, usually indifferent to anything that came out of Scotland, had praised him to the skies: 'A spiky challenging proletarian voice,' was the judgement of *The New Statesman*. 'Carnie tears aside the lace curtains to reveal the dark side of urban life' – that was *The Observer*. Others played the same tune. Only *The Scotsman's* reviewer – an elderly man known for his green velvet jackets and bow-ties – had expressed doubt. 'Mr Carnie's Scotland is recognizable only as an example of what may be called the urban kailyard. It is self-indulgent sentimentalism, scarcely disguised by a frenetic style.'

'Old ponce,' Carnie responded as he took off for London and fame and fortune. The fame withered quickly. The fortune never arrived. The last novel of the projected trilogy died on him. He wrote some plays which were staged but poorly received. He turned to journalism. A Sunday newspaper gave him a column where he was encouraged to express his prejudices. The paper, once popular, was losing circulation as its ageing readership died off and was not replaced. It was read by few intelligent people. Carnie was billed as 'The Voice of Sanity'. He excoriated the 'gutless' liberals of the Establishment and repeatedly explained how he had come to see through Socialism: 'being generous with other people's money'. He recalled the stern virtues of Presbyterian Scotland and deplored the decadence of his native land. The Scots, he told his mostly English suburban readers, had become a bunch of subsidy junkies and whingeing third-raters. When an indignant Labour politician denounced him as a 'self-hating Scot', he made this the subject of a column. 'I don't hate myself,' he wrote, 'I hate what my fellow-Scots have made of Scotland.'

'I really meant it,' he told me years later. 'I love Scotland. I just don't like to see it the way it is now.'

In the years of his column he sometimes still spoke of working on that third novel. Other times he grew angry if it was mentioned. Anger always came easily to him. I was a cub reporter on the paper. Then he picked me out as his assistant, researcher, gofer, what have you. I won't say we became close. Carnie kept colleagues at a distance, but I was closer than most. 'We speak the same language,' he said once, me being a Fifer. 'I'm a Calvinist atheist,' he said, 'you know what I mean. Most don't.' In the five years I worked with him or for him, he exhausted two marriages. Then I rose on the paper and his column was shunted off the op-ed page. He held that against me, though I wasn't responsible. Most of his day was now spent in El Vino's or the Telegraph's pub, a dismal place where there were always puddles of beer on the bar counter.

He had, still had, his coterie of admirers, groupies you would call them, mostly young, or not quite so young, men, and the occasional very pretty girl. The men lapped up his sour one-liners and bought him drinks. The girls longed to redeem him, save him from himself. They ironed his shirts, took his suits to the dry cleaner, helped him through hangovers. The more bitterly he snarled, the more he was cared for and revered, even if the number of admirers dwindled by the year. He lost quite a few when what became his most notorious one-liner went the rounds. 'Fucking Hitler, he made it impossible to say what you really think about the Jews'.

There were weeks when, though I was now a deputy editor, I wrote his column for him or re-wrote it making some sense of his rambling fulminations. Eventually there was a go of DT. A new editor sacked him. 'A good riddance, we've got to appeal to younger readers.' None, or very few, answered the appeal, but Carnie disappeared from the scene. It was years before I heard of him again, and I might have thought him dead if I didn't know he would have merited an obituary and none had appeared.

I came back north, as political editor of a new Sunday paper. There was a new spirit in the country. You could sniff optimism even in the Edinburgh air. The launch of the paper was proof, the editor assured me. 'It's a building-block of the New Scotland,' he said; he would repeat the sentence in his first leading article. I went along with it. Why not? It might even be true. Anyway that was the way the wind was blowing and I was happy to be carried along by it. The truth was, of course, my career in London had stalled. 'Westminster's played out,' I said, to excuse myself. And there was a girl in the case. There usually is. She was called Katie and she worked for a company that made documentaries. She had used me on one of them, and though I failed to get her into bed, we struck up a sort of friendship. So I came back to the New Scotland, even eagerly.

I had been in the job a couple of months when I got a call from a woman who had worked with me on the London paper. I assumed she wanted a job. Not at all, she said, she had exchanged journalism for motherhood, was married to a BBC producer of wildlife programmes and was back in Glasgow, living in the West End.

'It's not me,' she said, 'it's Adam.'

'Adam?'

'Adam Carnie.'

She had been one of his groupies. I'd forgotten. She may have been the shirt-ironer.

'Jesus Christ,' I said

'He's living with us just now. He very much wants to see you.'

'There's no job for him either, Margaret,' I said.

'That's not what he wants, but he does very much want to see you, needs to see you even.'

When I made no immediate reply, she said, 'He's not drinking. He's given that up.'

Margaret gave me a peck on the cheek and then, to my surprise, a hug.

'He's so pleased you agreed,' she said. 'You'll find him changed.'

Changed? Yes. For the better, was my first thought. There was more flesh on him and he looked serene. He gave me a smile and there was no malice in it. Margaret brought us coffee and scones and left us alone. We sat in the bay window looking out over Kelvingrove Park. The sun was shining and the trees, just turning, red, gold and brown, glistened after overnight rain.

'I owe Margaret a lot,' he said – I'd never known him acknowledge a debt to anyone. 'She's stopped me drinking. I couldn't have done it without her. And I'm working again.'

'The last book in the trilogy?' I said, not really thinking.

'Not that, no.' He didn't even seem offended by my suggestion.

'Not that, no,' he said again. 'Though I have an idea for it. She got me to AA, you know.'

'Christ,' I said, 'you're not writing about fucking Alcoholics Anonymous, not one of these how I emerged from misery and learned to love myself memoirs?'

He actually smiled, a nice smile, as if he was at ease with himself.

'No,' he said, 'it's Scotland and Me, an autobiographical history. I want you to find me a publisher – and serialize it in your paper. Needs livening up, that paper.'

Well, he was right there anyway. I mentioned it to the editor. He had never heard of Adam, but I persuaded him it might be something for us. He used to be good, I said, out of old loyalty. I didn't say: and he can write, unlike most of the wankers you've recruited.

I saw him a few times, had a couple of lunches with him, over the weeks that followed. He was serene, still not drinking, and said he was happy in his work. He looked trim. Margaret was probably still ironing his shirts.

Then the book arrived. It was well-written, quite unlike his old ranting column. It offered a keen appraisal of everything that had gone wrong in his life and in the history of modern Scotland. The theme was a refusal to look reality in the face and a preference for self-indulgent, self-pitying myth. It was profoundly depressing, but it was also good, even if, characteristically, he equated his failure with Scotland's.

The first three publishers refused it. One said it spilled all the dirt on Scotland. Eventually I found a small publisher who said he would do it if the author contributed to the costs of publication. I said I couldn't ask an author with Adam's distinguished history – I laid this on rather – to do that. He insisted. Eventually Margaret coughed up without telling Adam. I set to work to persuade my editor to run an extract. He demurred.

'Won't do us any good,' he said.

'It'll stir things up,' I replied, 'isn't that what you want, Derek?'

He compromised. He would run the piece with a critique by the paper's pet, a fashionable historian, alongside it. He was making it clear that the paper didn't endorse Adam's argument. Neat, I thought, bastard. It's take it or leave it, I said to Adam. He took it.

The historian was a smooth-jowled phoney. My opinion, not the general one. Newspaper editors and television producers loved him. His article was an exercise in one-upmanship and condescension. He shed crocodile tears over 'the wreck of a rare talent'; 'Mr Carnie may have arrived at self-understanding, but he knows nothing of modern Scotland' – that sort of thing. He ignored the real equation Adam made: between the self-delusion and bitter memories that had corrupted his own life and the self-delusion, false history and distorted memories in which, he said, the so-called New Scotland was indulging.

Then came the television debate, Adam and the historian, with

Molly Sprouston, confidante of Labour politicians and star interviewer of *Caledonian Television*, in the chair. Molly and the historian worked as a team. They'd been friends since Glasgow Uni days, more than friends by some accounts. They led and provoked Adam into wild talk, and exchanged pitying smiles. It was like a bear-baiting, with Adam tied to the stake.

'They set out to make a fool of me. I think they succeeded. Bastards.'

They did more than that. They destroyed him. He didn't go straight from the studio to the pub, but it wasn't long before he was there and drinking heavily again. He dropped out, refused to see even Margaret. Soon we didn't know where he was living or how.

It was months later I got a call from her.

'It's Adam,' she said, straightaway. 'He's dying. Liver failure and failure of other organs. He's in the Royal. He wants to see you, say goodbye, says it's urgent.'

Her voice broke up. She was weeping.

'All right,' I said. 'I'll go.'

He was in a bed by the window. The morning had been wet but a weak sun was pushing slowly through the clouds. The bed immediately opposite Adam's was empty.

'Aye, he went this morning,' Adam said, 'it's me next for the mortuary.'

I would have liked to contradict him, but he looked so wasted it was a wonder he was still talking.

'I asked Margaret to fetch you. He'll understand me, I said. I've been wrong all my life, but now we're in injury time, I've had an epiphany. You'll ken the word?'

I nodded and took hold of his hand. It was like gripping a skeleton.

'All my life I've gone with the flow and its bad memories and hatreds,' he said. He was speaking with difficulty. 'That's not the way to live. You have to swim upstream, let the past float away from you. Then you can hope. That's what I should have done, it's what Scotland has to do. That's all. Famous last words,' he said and closed his eyes.

I sat there for I don't know how long as the sun got brighter and fell golden-yellow on the bed and the sky turned blue.

Epiphany, I thought, that's the Feast of the Wise Men from the East, isn't it? Back home I got out the dictionary and read the secondary meaning:, 'sudden revelation or insight into the nature, essence or meaning of something.'

Adam's epiphany? Yes, perhaps, maybe.

# BORROWED LANDSCAPE

## Ronald Frame

A quarter-of-an-acre.

It's bare land, distant by only a shout from the shore.

She doesn't own it. 'No one owns anything,' her father used to say, 'except on paper.' He could have passed as a churchman, a minister, if he hadn't been a born atheist.

It won't be so easy for her to pay the rent, out of her pension and the few savings she has, but she'll find a way. The money she used to earn teaching at the school she would spend on books and records and all the foreign travel she did. The money went on broadening her mind, and she has no regrets about it now.

How could she have? Her mind is filled with pictures of all the places she's been. She has read thousands of books, and put in countless hours watching plays and films. She used to sit up in the gods at the opera, and stood along the walls in folk clubs, and sweated it out in jazz cellars.

It was money put to good use.

'Keep your outgoings to a minimum.' That had been her parents' mantra for good household management. And easier for her than for them, since she never married nor had a child to bring up.

'Make a life for yourself without servants or masters either.' She could have her freedom, her parents showed her. (Freedom with responsibility.) Her father used to quote Andre Gide; 'Accept nothing, question everything.'

That was the bedrock philosophy of Rob Urquhart, and his wife, and their friends, fellow socialist-activists like themselves.

Her father never became a 'traveller', a communist, although he might have been tempted at one time. Later he could say that communism had proved to be just another type of fascism.

Some kids had grown up with posters on the walls, and slogans spouted over the tea table. It had been a milder form of indoctrination in the Urquhart home: improving books out of the lending library, propped up against the side of the tea pot in its cosy – back copies of *Tribune* covering the holes in the rugs – a wireless set of their own, being paid up into infinity, and Beethoven's symphonies inextricably mixed in her memory with the neighbours' voices carrying up from the shared back green.

This was before the War, she had to remind young people, who had little idea of the past. It was in the days of masters and servants, all right, just before her father and his cronies got on their bikes and headed up to the Highlands, to take on the lord in his castle.

In fact it wasn't a lord they picked their quarrel with (*politely* picked it, her father always maintained), but the new owner of an old Perthshire estate – a Glasgow ironmaster, who had jumped over his older brothers and cousins to take command of the family firm.

'Right to roam,' she would say to young people, the ones she used to teach and some of whom became teachers themselves, inspired by her example: 'right of way, ramblers' access.' Bright as they were, they didn't know what she was talking about. They took it for granted that they could walk the moors and hike in the hills and pitch tents at lochsides and not need to ask permission. But that privilege had had to be won, thanks to like-minded pioneers first blazing a trail and holding their nerve as they did so.

The story wasn't all about heroism, though: it wasn't all about doughty victors and vanquished foes. Life is seldom that neat and tidy.

The ironmaster was to exact his revenge. He leaned on her father's employer, one of the Clyde shipbuilders, and a reason was found to serve Rob Urquhart with his notice. 'Your huff and bluff won't work with me, my man,' his boss barked at him.

Nor could it have helped her father that he was known as Red Rob among his fellow workers and the management.

From one of her father's dominie friends, Beak Thompson, she learned the expression 'Pyrrhic victory', and heard his patient explanation about Pyrrhus trouncing the Romans at the battle of Asculum but seeing the bulk of his own army decimated in the process. 'Another victory like this one will be our undoing.' Beak Thompson could be credited with having introduced her to classical history, which would retain its fascination for her through all the decades that followed until this one, the second of the next century.

She can't consider her quarter-acre of land, her bare garden-to-be on the coast, windswept and salt-sprayed, and not think of her father.

She can't return the several hundred yards from the quarter-acre field

to her roadside cottage and not think of her mother, somehow convert-
ing that wooden cabin in the bracken foothills outside Glasgow, among the
several dozen identical green-painted cabins with tin roofs, into a welcoming refuge, the Urquharts' dacha for weekends and holidays. Several times
they had put up guests, unknown to her and deliberately kept as strangers, never referred to by name so that she wouldn't be able to identify
them if asked to by the police. (Her parents, both of them, had instilled
into her the notion that truth came first, the paragon virtue – and even
if truth was sometimes best served by a lie, the lie shouldn't come out of
a child's mouth.)

Her mother wasn't a self-taught naturalist like her father, and never got
to recognise the different bird calls or animals tracks. But she became adept
at foraging for berries and nuts and wild herbs, which all added piquancy
and stylishness to their meals in the cabin.

Her mother got the hang of goulash and pilaff, and was a dab hand
with a ragout, when those terms were virtually unknown, certainly where
they came from in Clydebank. They once accommodated a Parisian, a shop
steward from one of the big motor factories there – yes, he definitely *was*
a Moscow die-hard, a collectivist – who left them as a thank-you present
a French iron casserole, which still sat on *her* dresser today. Mealtimes
in Glasgow sometimes involved identifying how many countries on her
revolving globe had contributed to this repast.

Long tram rides up to the city had taken them to the Art Galleries at
Kelvingrove, where she found the wider world waiting for her in one
marble-floored room after another: paintings, statues, artefacts religious
and secular, stuffed animals and birds, suits of armour, fossils, mechanical
inventions, costumes. Glasgow felt as if it was at the centre of the world.
Last of all on their Kelvingrove visits they looked at the Glasgow Boys
paintings: those young artists of the 1880s and 1890s had brought back
their impressions of abroad and made the everyday *here* look just a little
different – so that she, young Nan Dempsey, would feel she was having to
learn to recognise the familiar all over again.

Now her life belongs in a museum, some folk think. Or to a half-hour
TV doc, or to a module in an FE study course. To them Nan Dempsey's life
is all about the past.

But sometimes, frequently in fact, she feels that *that* time was more alive
and NOW, it was more fully lived, than *this* present time ever is.

Her own living and breathing present is worth more to her because of
the past lives and experiences that are bound up with it.

Another matter –

Why does she feel that she was more 'Scottish' then, with a surer idea of Scotland's place in the big wide world? When did people's minds start to narrow?

Even at the age she is, well through her eighth decade, Nan Dempsey is making discoveries.

She has gone back to first principles so often, *because* she has studied all the other possibilities and permutations. She inclines wherever she can to the simple and uncomplicated, to the clear-cut.

At sixty she hit on Tao and Zen, alighting on what she already knew without realising that she knew it.

Yin and yang, balance, equilibrium.

Go with the flow.

Resist a hostile force (as in martial arts) by turning it back on itself. (Project your foot and trip up your assailant, send him flying.)

Don't withstand nature, don't deny the inevitable.

For years she worked on her allotment strips, her little basement areas and back yards, anywhere she could lay her hands on.

She followed the gardening experts, so-called, who were mostly writing for a Southern English audience. Stupidly she didn't think things out for herself. She tried to grow plants which it took her far too long to understand don't like the Scottish weather.

Don't blame the climate or your bad judgement.

Follow nature.

In her quarter-acre she is going to have only indigenous planting. (It's so blindingly obvious to her now: the truth was staring her in the face all along.) She will grow only what grows in these parts already.

SHE WILL CULTIVATE A WILD GARDEN.

From her scrapbook of newspaper cuttings:

*There's an expression in garden design called 'a borrowed landscape'. If you're lucky enough to have a decent-sized garden but want to make it seem bigger, and if you live somewhere rural with open land around you – then you remove all or part of a boundary hedge or wall, eliminating that distinction between your garden and what is beyond it. You've borrowed a view, and brought it into your garden – or rather, you've allowed your own garden to spill over its limits and appear to go on and on.*

On her quarter-acre there is an unkempt redcurrant thicket she plans to take up, and a dying rowan to be felled. She will sacrifice those, and not lose sleep over their loss. That will give her an uninterrupted view, out across open water. Her garden will seem to have no borders now, no restrictions, nothing to constrain it.

Her father wouldn't ever talk about the bad times. Her mother had been less reticent, and didn't conceal the fact that she had *not* forgiven those who boasted about seeing Red Rob cut down to size.

Two of the children ended up going north (she, Nan, and brother Eric), early on one (older brother Steve) headed as far from Scotland as possible – New Zealand, while the fourth (sister Ella) chose to stay on in Glasgow.

Nan turned into the eco-warrior of the four.

And it was *she* who would be called 'arty', she who now realises that art doesn't have to be innovative, edgy, challenging all the time. (*Distrust the shibboleths!* she knows.) Art is also about recording, about giving voice to a way of life that is becoming outmoded, which is being erased from public consciousness.

Her own upbringing, for instance.

She was inculcated with a strict moral code, for all her parents' free thinking. She had the Scots work ethic beaten into her, literally, at school. But by the time she reached adulthood, the world had moved on, and she was left defined by values that went unappreciated by others.

Nan Dempsey? Och, she's too serious-minded, yon one: too formal, too frugal, not flexible enough. Too old-fashioned altogether.

While she would come to see that change was unavoidable, she was also left feeling cheated. She continually had to fight against her own sharp tongue and a bent for sarcasm. That intolerance with things only mellowed in middle age. She was kept waiting rather a long time, but finally she did become her own person, confident inside her own skin – once her parents had passed away, within a year of each other. It was because *they* weren't here that she knew she had to keep herself up to the mark: no longer needing to please, no longer despairing whenever she fell short, she could concentrate instead on harvesting all of her natural talents.

About gardening she is self-taught.

Her father thought gardens were an urban bourgeois invention, while her mother was one for the marigolds and busy-lizzies.

Where her own horticulturist's eye comes from, and the green fingers, she has no idea. She used to read all the gardening articles in the weekend newspapers, and in the shops she sped-read books she couldn't afford to buy, and that was how she acquired her know-how.

Encyclopaedic, in a word.

And here is the curious upshot: she had to learn so much only in order to unlearn it again and get back to those first principles.

She will have her borrowed landscape.

The inlet of sea, the blue mountains beyond.

And, beyond *that*, there is to be ... the borrowed landscape of the past.

Not the past of history books, but the portable one inside her head. People, places, the small incidents which sometimes went on to have big consequences.

She will grow the native species, pruning and controlling them, but knowing that unlike her earlier endeavours, these shrubs and trees and grasses have a much better chance of survival. No exotics, no ornamentals, the minimum of herbaceous. Instead: reliable Scots roses, scented and free flowering even if they don't repeat – and tough-as-old-boots yellow broom – the pine species sylvestris, with reddish bark and grey leaves – trusty, bright green shield ferns. Whatever she plants will have to justify its presence, earn its keep. She won't humour the temperamentals, she simply doesn't have the energy that requires.

She can't hang around, either, waiting and waiting for what will come into its own in twenty years' time. Someone else will get the benefit of her foresight.

A garden, they say, is also the gardener's own history.

*This* plant was a surreptitious cutting, *that* plant was a gift or a spur-of-the-moment purchase.

A garden speaks of its maker's aspirations, or the lack.

A garden hints at somewhere else, in glimpses.

A brackeny hillside, for instance. A line of flat-topped pines, like the crest near Aberfoyle where her father always claimed he'd met her mother, where the cyclists paused to rest.

Her father used to sport an outsized purple rhododendron flower as a trophy, every time he passed by the ironmaster's estate, but she was in two minds about introducing a rhododendron bush to her quarter-acre. The purple rhoddie was wild now, and a thug like that in the garden doesn't know when to stop.

About the rest she is clear enough. A *Scottish* garden, one without favour from the Gulf Stream, one without stone walls. She will root a windbreak of sorts where the Atlantic elements blow straight in, on the west flank, never mind that she won't live long enough to see its usefulness. Or perhaps, conceivably, an equinoctial gale – the sort where a genie shatters his bottle and escapes – will dig it up again before it has even got going.

The weather is in a state of flux. In recent years these parts have received less sun, more wind, more rain, heavier snowfalls. She has no idea why it is happening. The blasts power the windmills, which – like Don Quixote – she has tilted at, hoping against hope to block the planning permits.

You can't stop the world from doing what it is intent on doing. Even so, 'Don't accept something lying down – unless you're lying down to protest,' so her father told her, in her own Faslane days. But also, 'Know when to pick yourself up again.'

Don't let your defeats defeat *you*. Make do, try your best, accommodate yourself – then move on to the next cause.

What is the alternative, if she wants to consider herself a woman of conscience and integrity? (Smugness is a besetting vice of the Scots, like sentimentality, but she's always had her siblings and her friends and her pupils to help keep her feet set firmly, squarely, on the ground.)

Lying in bed last thing, she goes through a list of what to get hold of.

> Pink-purple hardy geranium sylvaticum
> Moonraker sedge
> Saxifrage oppositifolia
> Elder, or sambucus nigra
> Wood rush
> Lythrum, purple loosestrife
> Buckler fern
> Salix, the willow
> Blue-green quaking grass

The garden has already been made, inside her head, and she dreams of it at night.

A garden can't ever be completed, though. A gardener never sees just what is there in front of her. She can't be still, something always requires doing. A gardener is happily cursed to perpetual motion.

*She didn't wake one morning, the day she was due to begin work on her garden. That garden of hers was always such a crazy idea anyway.*

She starts awake from her bad dream, still hearing the words of her sister Ella's typed, businesslike letter to her friends. She stares ahead of her into the darkness. It's the middle of the night. She must get up.

The cottage isn't normally cold, but it feels cold now. Even when she's sitting by the stove, she can't get warm enough.

The dream has shaken her.

Since retiring here, she's become conversant with the local lore and legends. The mystical atmosphere appealed to her from the outset.

Now and then she has wondered why it happened so easily, that the plot of ground was available to her. At once she was able to spot its potential: that view, out across the inlet, to the misted peaks beyond. Even in summer, it's said, frozen snow fills gulches just below their summits.

Who else before her, across aeons of time, appreciated that this view was so special?

Only a couple of generations ago, they used to speak hereabouts of the mysterious Isles of the Blest, or Paradise, which lay just over the sea's horizon. People would talk about 'being summoned', 'gathered' for the journey there.

Her old teaching friends, in good health and content with home comforts, used to laugh when she went back to the town to see them and told them what she was up to.

'I'm thinking of making myself a garden,' she announced to them, not mentioning that she had signed a long-term rental agreement with the estate office. Nor did she let on that the expression on the face of the factor's young assistant as he waved her off from his door confirmed he thought she was cracked.

She moves as close to the stove as she can, wrapping the tartan rug closer about her – just like an old crone by her peat fire in one of those island tales.

With the curtains at the window pulled back, she sits on the chair looking out. Her eyes naturally trace a route to the site of her planned garden.

And it is *now*, for the first time in her eight years here in this community, it's now that she sees it – THE GREEN RAY!

It reaches out of the night sky, the mythical bridge to day. Across that slender plane of communication, the path of flashing light in darkness, pass the living and the dead.

She could never believe in its existence – but there it is! The greenness brightens in intensity, till it has the brilliance of phosphorescence.

The effect lasts for no more than a few seconds. An optical phenomenon perhaps, but she can't remember having seen, even on all her gallivanting to foreign lands, anything so spectacular or quite so beautiful.

She was sitting upright in the chair, still wrapped in her rug and with her eyes open, when they found her the following afternoon.

She must have been in that position, dead, for at least twelve hours.

She was clutching some sheets of paper, still held in the tight grip of both hands.

What were they? Just freehand drawings of a garden – a rough layout – 'suggested plantings'. Nothing more important than that.

Even when her hands had been opened and the fingers prised apart, the pages could only be extricated with difficulty. It was as if she was resisting everyone, to the very last: as if the sad old woman had thought she might actually have some precious, invaluable secret to guard!

# THE TRANSFORMATION

## Allan Radcliffe

He appeared on a Monday in early December. I was at the counter tying on my apron, late for my shift, a little flustered. He blew through the door and stood for a moment, stamping his long legs and blowing into his hands. Snow from his boots gathered on the welcome mat.

He hovered at the door, scanning the room, eyes widening as they bounced between the tables of men of different heights and ages and shapes. I knew what he was thinking: could he make a clean getaway without anyone noticing? Walk down the street and find somewhere straight, a Starbucks maybe? He turned to the window. Outside the snow was horizontal. He took a few faltering steps into the room and lowered himself into a chair, forcing the sharp points of his knees under the table.

The door banged frequently, the tables filling with familiar faces. Service would be brisk until around two. Then peace and quiet, cleaning up and counting the clock round until closing. Bobby was picking me up at six.

'What can I get you?'

He peered out from behind the menu. His hair was a shade of white so pure it seemed almost artificial, thick, combed back from his face and shaved at the sides. Neatly sculpted sideburns framed his fine, even features.

'I'm going to have a pot of tea and one of these' – his mouth quirked – '*special* club sandwiches.'

I scratched the order into my pad, pleasantly surprised. The passing trade, the ones who didn't have time to flee before I took their order, usually 'just have the filter coffee'. They downed it and then they paid up and walked out. You never saw them again.

His eyes were dark-brown, almost black, and huge against the stretched brown parchment of his skin. I took his menu. He looked about him, taking in the wood panelling, the red-brick walls and the oily landscapes in the fluorescent frames. His face suddenly creased, his eyes disappearing under a busy network of lines. He looked away and fell into a convulsion of laughter. The laughter pushed right to the edge of his breath until he was hunched over making a kind of choking noise. I wondered if he was drunk. I wondered if I should stay there smiling politely or call for backup.

'Sorry,' he said, his voice a watery squeak as though he'd been crying. 'It's just. This place.' He rubbed his eyes. 'You know what this building used to be?'

'I – This building?' When I was at school I wasn't allowed down this end of town, by the river. Mum and Dad had heard stories. But that was years ago, long before the clean-up. 'It was a – shop that sold suits, a tailor, I think.'

'No, I'm talking *way* back.' He flapped a hand over his shoulder. 'Fifty years ago this place was a house of ill repute. A hotel for gentleman travellers.' He leaned forward. '*A knocking shop.*'

I smiled, unsure what to say. The throaty laughter followed me all the way back to the counter. His voice resonated in my head as I wrestled with the coffee machine. I couldn't place his accent. There was something Scottish buried deep in there – a faint rolling of the 'r'; the occasional flat vowel sound. But his voice went up at the end of the sentence as though he were asking a question.

I took him his coffee. His black overcoat hung over the back of his chair and a black suit hung loose from his narrow shoulders. His neck muscles where they met the top of his shirt reddened as he drew back to let me set the milk jug on the table.

'Thank you, my friend.' He coughed hard. 'I apologise for my, uh, hysteria right now. I'm a little tired. Hell of a morning –'

'One of those days, eh?'

'I've just buried my mother.' He lowered his eyes.

'I'm sorry to hear that.' I felt my face colouring.

He snorted, 'You didn't know her,' and seemed to instantly recognise the wrongness of his comment. 'Thank you, my friend, that's very kind.' A pause. 'Are you a native of this town?'

'Am I –?' I hugged the tray to my chest. 'I was born here.'

'What age are you?'

'Twenty-six.'

'Student?'

'I was.' I hesitated. 'I'm on a break. That's why I came back here.' I shifted my weight from foot to foot. More than a year on I was still too ashamed to admit I'd screwed up my finals.

'Haven't decided what to do with your life yet.' His voice went up at the end again, but it wasn't a question.

'Something will come up.'

'Well, don't sit around too long waiting for something to land in your lap, my friend.'

My hands tightened around the tray. I could feel my lips twitching in anger. I fled for the counter. When the club sandwich appeared in the hatch I asked my colleague Greg to take it over to him.

The café started emptying. The sun came out. Light shone through the window, cutting across the old man's face. He ordered another pot of tea and a slice of cheesecake and sat for the rest of the afternoon gazing out the window. Best seat in the house. The café sat right on the corner at the top of the hill. On a clear day you could see all the way down to the river.

Every so often, as the sun shifted, the old man moved his chair round to keep his face in the light. Greg nudged me and nodded in the direction of the window. 'Do you think he's moving in?'

When my back was turned, I caught him watching me in the mirror that hung over the counter. His eyes were large and dark and troubled. Part of me wished he would invite me to sit with him, that he would ask me more blunt, impertinent questions. It seemed funny, the two of us alone in this small space, separated by the counter, not speaking, barely acknowledging each other's presence.

He finally left around four. When I went to clear his table there were two towers of pound coins next to his empty cup. I counted it up. It was three times the price of his order.

He came back late the next morning. Sat at the same spot by the window and arranged his things on the table: a laptop, mobile phone, a couple of books and a newspaper. He ordered the club sandwich and drank pot after pot of tea. Every so often his mobile would ring and he would talk loudly into it, bombarding whoever was on the other end with questions about what he was missing back home.

I drifted close to his table and overheard him advising a friend to get his finger out and start looking for a proper job. He was sick of hearing his friend's excuses. No wonder the friend was depressed. There was a murmur of protest on the other end of the line, but the old man was unmoved. No more excuses. 'The rest of us have to put in a day's work – what makes you so special?'

Later, when he came over to pay, I tried not to notice the way his hand shook as he flustered with his wallet.

He raised an eyebrow as he handed over his money.

'A smile costs nothing. You ever hear that expression?'

I laughed, in spite of myself.

Today he was wearing a loose black shirt, open almost to the waist with a white T-shirt underneath that fitted him like a second skin. A chunky silver chain hung around his neck. When he noticed me admiring it he told me he had bought it in a flea market in San Francisco.

'San Francisco? You live there?'

'For the past fifty-odd years. Have you been, Neil?'

I blinked, surprised he knew my name.

'One day. Maybe.'

He let go his crackly half-laugh, half-cough. 'You shouldn't think too hard about these things. Just go.' He leaned forward. 'You can wait tables in Frisco too, you know?'

As he turned to go I asked his name.

'My name is Terence.' He spoke slowly, carefully, like he was making an announcement. 'I'll see you tomorrow, Neil.'

The following day Terence seemed subdued. He walked more slowly than usual. He seemed his age suddenly. There was no chatter when I went over to take his order. He sat in his favourite spot with his face tipped towards the sun. He opened his newspaper and let his eyes float over the pages, as though trying to detach himself from the bustle around the counter. Later he sat hunched over the table, his fingers curled territorially around his cup.

I went over to clear his table. He gestured at me to sit down.

'I'm flying home tomorrow.'

'To San Francisco? Will you come back?'

'I can't imagine coming back.' He looked at me for a moment then turned to the window. 'Do you see that office block, right down at the end of the street?' I leaned forwards. 'By the railway bridge. You see?'

'It's an insurance company.'

'Fifty years ago there was a restroom down there. A convenience. You know, a public toilet.' He narrowed his eyes at me. 'Only, no one went there to use the toilet, if you know what I mean.'

I turned to look out the window. That office block by the railway bridge suddenly seemed so clean and scrubbed and new looking it almost gleamed.

'When I left school I got a job with a firm that sold screws and nails. Yeah, you can imagine: soul-numbing stuff.' He sighed. 'I'd heard that you could meet queers down by the river, in that place, after dark. So one Friday night when I'd had a few beers I went down. It was pitch-black inside – they used to take out the light bulbs.' He closed his eyes. 'I can still remember that feeling of sheer terror in my stomach when I saw someone moving towards me in the dark.'

He sat back in his seat, his face tightening. 'We used to take turns standing guard, but people got complacent. One night the police raided. I got six months in what they used to call the bad boys' home.'

'How old were you?'

'Sixteen. When I came out my mother, my brothers – well, they didn't want to know me.'

'So – that's when you went away?'

'I went to London first. Worked in a hotel kitchen. Then I found out that this big Californian hotel chain was recruiting. I worked my way up to sous chef, executive sous chef then chef.' He sighed. 'On my thirty-fifth birthday I used my savings to start my own catering business.'

Terence was looking just past me as he said all this, a v-shaped groove carved into his forehead. But he wasn't bragging. He reeled off his achievements mechanically, as though ticking off a checklist in his head, reminding himself of the path he had taken.

He turned to me. 'I took a walk down by that part of the river yesterday morning –'

'That must have been – interesting.'

'Sometimes I wonder what would have happened to me if I hadn't been arrested that night.' He smiled. 'Maybe I would still be working for a company that sells screws and nails.'

Bobby was waiting for me after work. We kissed on the street and defiantly held hands on the short walk to his flat. We ate and settled down to watch television. A film came on but I quickly lost the thread. We spooned on the sofa and Bobby did his best to explain what was happening, his voice slipping animatedly over my shoulder as I tried to stay focused on the screen.

'Bobby?'

'Mmn?'

'Do you remember what you were like when you were sixteen?'

'Sixteen?' He thought for a moment. 'I was a clown. When you're one of six you'll do almost anything to get attention.'

'Did you know you were gay?'

'Oh *yeah*. Tried not to think about it, though. Whenever I had a quiet moment – you know, when I was in the bath or lying in bed – and it came back to me that I was one of those, a *jessie*, it made me feel, well – *lonely*.'

He lifted the remote and muted the sound on the television.

'What about you?'

I rolled my eyes back in my head. I didn't remember much about my teenage years. Whenever I thought back to what school was like, it felt like a slow submersion in dark, dirty water.

I remembered once, I must have been sixteen or thereabouts, going along to a pub on the High Street one Saturday night. My friends pushed me to the bar – my height meant it was easier for me to get served. At chucking out time, as we spilled out into the street, a fight broke out somewhere behind us. It spread like a virus until there was a mass of people, drunk and angry, swaying as one across the street. I suddenly found myself stuck right down in the middle of it. The violence, the noise was infectious. I began to push back with my chest, my shoulders.

At some point a drunken voice landed in my ear. 'Hey queer! You left your handbag in the pub!' Anger went through me like a line of fire. I turned around. The man was young, red-eyed with the drink. I squared up to him. I shoved him hard in the chest. I shoved him again, this time so hard he fell off the pavement and landed in a heap in the gutter, his mouth hanging open, his eyes confused. I turned and pushed my way out of the crowd. I walked quickly away, breathless, exhilarated.

I squeezed Bobby's hand.

'You know, I think I was less of a coward back then. I used to think people got braver with age. Now I'm not sure.' I looked down at the half-empty bottle of wine on the floor and smiled. 'So, if you came face to face with your teenage self, what would you say?'

He tilted his head. 'Oh, who knows – lots of things: contradictory things. I'd tell him to relax. Have more fun. Take school more seriously. I'd tell him not to wear those god awful drainpipe jeans to his cousin's wedding. I'd – I'd tell him that life will be hard sometimes but – well, you know.' He shrugged. 'What about you?'

I just lay there not knowing what to say. Something inane came on television that took Bobby's attention and the moment passed. I was thinking about Terence, high above the Atlantic, picking restlessly at his airline meal, frowning impatiently at the movie. I closed my eyes and tried to imagine the sixteen-year-old Terence sorting through his screws and nails on the factory floor. I pictured him standing at the production line sorting keen-eyed through boxes dense with pins and tacks. A self-contained figure: industrious, determined, the expression on his face impenetrable.

# VALUES WE CAN GET BEHIND

## Benjamin Werdmuller

Buy. Create. Share. Build. Sell.

They painted the words in red on the wall opposite the subway station platform as a kind of positive reinforcement, I suppose. I remember the days when they used to advertise products and services in the subway, or when some charity or other would drum up the money to post up a poem or a painting they thought people would enjoy. That hasn't been true since they worked out that advertising was much more effective if they beamed it to our devices and had a conversation with us, and that people just ignored the ones you just read or watched and weren't forced to interact with. So when advertising started to talk to us and expected us to talk back, the spaces that had been ads were used to try and instil a sense of purpose into us. We all know it's a kind of propaganda, but if you stare at a message for long enough, one day there it is anyway, running around in your head with all your other ideas.

In the old days, someone would have added something snarky in the conspicuous space at the end. That was in the days before they changed the law, though, and we left the final word alone: in sky blue, shining out like a window to the outside world. 'Community.'

This particular morning, which was one of those January mornings when you actually welcome the heat of the subway commute, I read it with fresh eyes. It had gone right back to being as cheesy as it was the first day I saw it, as ridiculous as all the people around me in their business suits or neat little sweaters, waiting to catch the train and start their ten hours of prescribed time in some focus grouped office somewhere.

They solved traffic a long time ago. It turns out that if all the cars on the road go at a particular speed, you don't get any traffic jams or accidents, and everyone gets to their destination faster. It's a more efficient way of doing it, and everyone agreed that if we could find a way to enforce that on the roads, there'd be less pollution, people would spend less time on their commutes, and everyone would lead happier lives. A company out in California found a way to make cars drive themselves, so they installed them in every new car, retrofitted the old ones, and no-one was allowed to drive anymore.

And then they solved us. We all started going online and filling out these public profiles that told everyone all about us, back when you could talk to anyone and they hadn't split the network into all the different National Internets. Social networking it was called, and first it was just for making friends and meeting people to do business with. But then they started linking things into the profiles: updating them when we bought something, or met up with our friends, or read a book.

Eventually they had these detailed files, more detailed than anything that had ever been collected about anyone, and they were about *everyone*; every single person in the world. It turned out that everyone has what they called a 'very best job', which was a back-handed way of saying a job where they'd do the most productive work and make the most money. And then it turned out that the only really good way to make the whole thing work efficiently was to make sure everyone was doing their very best jobs, so they installed the software in every company in the country, and no-one was allowed to choose their own jobs anymore.

Mostly, if truth be told, it wasn't so bad – at least, not for most people. It also turned out that people are most productive when they're happy, so people were pretty pleased with the arrangement. 'Choice is stressful,' the app companies used to say, so they built tools that made the best choices for us. Schools, jobs, business partners, lovers, husbands, wives, where you lived and who you met down the pub after work on a Friday night; no matter what kind of decision you had to make, there was an app for that, installed at the very highest levels and in the fabric of everything all around us.

So there I was, on that subway platform on a January morning, looking at all the people waiting for the train and trying to guess what job they'd been given, where they had been assigned to live, what the algorithms might say about their profiles. I could have picked up my handset and found out, of course. Some people even had head-up displays that told them everything they needed to know about a person as they spoke to them; names, previous conversations, the whole shebang. But not me. I liked to guess, and remember, and form a first impression using just a feeling. Even if I was wrong, it made me feel like I was alive.

The thing was, everyone around me seemed to be becoming less and less alive, at least as far as I could see. They were spoon-fed by the apps and their prescribed lives, and I couldn't ever quite get the hang of it. I tried, don't get me wrong; I didn't see what else I could do other than try and fit in and do what they wanted me to do. It seemed to be making everyone so happy, and I wanted to be happy too.

As much as I hated to admit it, what made me happiest was thinking and deciding for myself. It was a disadvantage: I knew my choices were going to be less efficient than the ones the apps made for me. I knew I'd be poorer, and wouldn't be as happy. I thought I'd probably never find a girlfriend, let alone someone who would tolerate my whims and mood swings for my whole life. But I couldn't help it. This was me, and the harder I tried to suppress it, the harder my emotions came out swinging – and with them, my egotistical self-determination and my misery.

The truth was, I wasn't on that subway platform to go to work. I was there to step out under the train and just end it there, for good. As I stood there looking at the crowd, my eyes darting around their faces while I guessed their lives, I was wondering how they could bear it. I began to doubt if they were even people anymore – happy, but bereft of free will or human spirit – or if I was missing some crucial aspect of my own humanity.

The wind on the platform picked up into a gust. I could feel the electricity in the air, and the hair on the back of my neck began to bristle. I absent-mindedly licked my lips. My eyes watered. And I began to push my way through the crowd, towards the bright yellow of the platform edge, holding my breath, my hands clutched tightly into fists –

'Scotia.'

Just a whisper, right at the edge of my hearing.

I stopped dead. The train rushed in front me, sending my hair flying while I stood, wide-eyed but alive.

'Scotia.'

There it was again; whispered but urgent, right at the edge of my hearing. I turned around and looked up and down the platform. It was empty; everyone had got on the subway train but me. There was nobody here.

'Scotia.'

I know now that they find the people who aren't conforming to their expected profiles and transmit through the notification networks in an undetectable way. The whispers are just below the range where the error detection algorithms will decide there's a problem; to them, it's just noise, even if the brain knows better. So it's a tactic, a way of helping people free themselves. But right then, in that moment, it felt like magic. Or madness, as much as there's a difference between the two.

I turned around and walked out through the station entrance onto deserted streets. Nobody would be here until the next commuter wave, which wasn't due for another twenty minutes. There was no litter, no food rotting in the gutter, nobody sitting on the pavement; there hadn't been for years. It felt like one of the old movies that used to show up in my 'Recommended For You' channel about the end of the world, where there's nobody left on earth except our hero, and he has to somehow survive after everybody else is dead and buried.

It took me a few minutes to see the sticker: small and black, carefully pasted to the bottom right of the frame on a poster so as not to trigger the aesthetic improvement algorithms running behind the cameras at the station. The writing was black too, but it caught the light differently to the background, so you could just about see the words if you peered at it from the right angle.

Scotia.

That was it; one word. No instructions, no attribution, nothing to say who had printed it or why.

It seemed like a funny word to choose. Scotia. Latin for Scotland.

I hadn't thought about Scotland for a long time, but it used to be one of those places that everyone knew. It hadn't done well in the recession; at least, it hadn't walked out with a whole lot of money, which a lot of people blamed on their having left the United Kingdom. I remembered reading about it at the time; when the apps and the mandatory profiles came in, the government algorithms decided that it would be more efficient for it to be spun off again as its own country, and that everyone would wind up happier. But the global financial markets had collapsed when each country got its own super-profile and the algorithms began to take over, and by the time everyone had picked themselves off the floor a few months later it sounded like Scotland wasn't doing very well at all. I hadn't heard anything else about it since then. But now here was this sticker, and the voice.

The clouds had cleared, and I looked around to see if I could see another sticker reflecting in the sun. After a while the crowds for the next commute began to trickle onto the street, and they must have thought I was mad, looking at all the posters and the struts of all the buildings at odd angles to see if I could see anything glinting in the light. I couldn't, so I combed my hair back into place and joined them, rubbing my eyes as I walked back into the station.

They played music on the subway trains, through the notification network so that each person heard whatever song the algorithms decided would make them the most productive. The music everyone else had been listening to was published on their profiles, of course, and for most people it was the same playlist every day; a part of their routines as much as brushing their teeth or putting on a tie. Mine was always different, but usually a song I knew, something that fit the mood the algorithm had decided I was in today. This one was a piece I'd never heard before – a simple tune sung by a man with a guitar. Something about a farm. I hung onto the ceiling strap, listening, and stared out at the blackness as it flew past: pipes and wires leading to places unknown, each playing its unseen part to keep the trains running and the commuter waves running to schedule.

I kept expecting to see a secret passageway embedded in the tunnel side, or a sticker peering out from the subterranean murk, but no such thing turned up. The music played, and the endless pipes and wires snaked across the encrusted walls of the commuter rat run, and I kept on standing.

I didn't hear the voice again, and I never saw another sticker. I diligently stuck to my commuter wave, day after day, standing on the platform with all the others, always keeping my eyes bright and my face up, but never forgetting the idea.

Scotia. It stood for something new to me: a place for the people who couldn't be held tight to a schedule or be sorted by an algorithm. Each morning, I stood on the platform and examined my fellow travellers, no longer wondering who they were or where they went to work, but asking questions like: What were they dreaming? Were they, too, desperate for the freedom that was burning inside me? How could just a sticker and a voice set so much of me alight?

It took me years to get out. There were no flights, or trains, or roads: I had to turn myself sideways and fit through the cracks in the algorithm, breaking away little by little. I threw my profile off the scent with an out-of-character movement one day, an off-key remark the next, until suddenly, without me expecting it or asking, it just let me go. I just got up one morning and walked away from the commuter train station, bang in the opposite direction, and kept on walking, finding my way north using the sun. They locked up my credits on the first day – I waved my device in front of the pay point at a supermarket, and nothing happened – so I'm ashamed to say I picked peoples' pockets, taking their handsets and abusing the crimeless trust the algorithm had established in all of us so that I could eat.

Nobody welcomed me when I got here. That wasn't the point, or the reason why I came. I didn't want to be accepted into a faceless group. I wanted to be me, free to be alone or sad or obsessed when I wanted to be. Don't get me wrong, though; there's community here, that's for certain. It supports us as individuals and respects us as who we are: flawed, inefficient, but alive.

I think sometimes about those words on the subway wall back where I came from: Buy, Create, Share, Build, Sell. Nobody designed that way of thinking. It evolved innocently into a trap that crushed our humanity in the name of making life better. All the people who oil the machines and polish the cogs are innocents too. All we do, me and the people here, is give them the seed of an idea: Scotia. But it's up to them to choose.

# WELCOME TO THE HOTEL CALEDONIA

## Peter Arnott, Alan Bissett, David Greig, Rona Munro, Morna Pearson & Alan Wilkins

To mark the elections to the Scottish Parliament in 2011 the Traverse Theatre in Edinburgh commissioned seven playwrights to work collaboratively on a play that would be performed on one day only – Thursday 5 May, Polling Day.

The writers decided at an early stage to locate the work in a fictional hotel, somewhere in Scotland, but waited until the two days before performance until they began to write it. This allowed them to make contemporary references to events in the immediate memory of the audience. And the deadline frightened the hell out of them and the performers.

The play was performed by Barrie Hunter, Andrew Scott Ramsay and Ashley Smith. With Director, David Greig, Stage Manager, Dan Dixon, Assistant Director, David Betz-Heinemann and Literary Assistant, Jennifer Williams.

Characters (*in order of appearance*)

**Svetlana**, the receptionist
**Manager**
**Gavin**, a local
**Drunk and Exhausted Writers**, five of them
**Woman in White**, hotel ghost
**Boy**, a wee chancer
**Wedding Guest**, a man
**Woman**, a wedding guest
**Man**, a wedding guest
**Mother**, of the groom
**Father**, of the groom
**Dad**, Father of the Bride
**Bride**

*All the scenes take place in the hotel, at some point in the future. A wedding is taking place.*

*A hotel reception desk is located centrally with stools and the paraphernalia usually found in a hotel lobby. There is a tingy reception bell on the desk. There are several raised and lit areas off the central desk that can be used for assorted reception rooms, bars and bedrooms. Images of Scottish icons and kitsch are projected above the main set as the audience enter.*

# SCENE 1
# THE HOTEL CALEDONIA

*The Hotel Reception. The Eagles song, Hotel California, plays. Song fades out as the lights rise. The performers enter, singing, and take up positions around the reception desk.*

**All** *(singing, to the tune of Hotel California)*
On a dark highland B road
Dreich mist in your hair
Slight smell of damp sheep shit
Rising up through the air.

Up ahead in the distance
You see a shimmering light
Your head feels heavy, you really need a drink
You'll have to stop for the night

Antlers hung in the doorway
You ting the reception bell
And you are thinking to yourself
This could be heaven or this could be hell.

Her face looks totally hostile
As she shows you the way
There are voices in the corridor
I think I hear them say ...

**Svetlana** *(spoken)* Welcome to the Hotel Caledonia.

**All** Such a lovely place

**Svetlana** My name is Svetlana.

**All** Such a lovely face

**Svetlana** Enough! Decadent western fools!

**Manager** Sorry.

**Svetlana** I have got to get out of this hotel. 6pm – time to turn on the TV. Ha. Election day. The day we dare to dream. And then tomorrow we wake up. That's politics. Let me tell you a story about politics.

My mother – when she was a young girl at the soviet school in Vilnius was asked by her teachers to write a speech about the values in which she truly believed. She immediately wrote a passionate speech about how as a young woman in the Soviet Union she had no need of the commodified distractions of western culture – no need for pop music or fashion or sexual promiscuity. She said young Soviet women should be energized by their role as equal citizens of a republic whose hopeful eyes were forever turned towards the dawning light of a brighter future. She was sensational. She was invited to deliver her speech to a congress of soviet youth in Moscow where she repeated her success. Then she went on a tour of the east. Moscow, Samarkand, Tblisi ... Finally, she was selected by the party to represent young soviet womanhood at a morale boosting rally of conscripts in a camp deep in the bleak wilderness of Kamchatka – where the Red Army stood eternally ready to defend our revolution from the sino leftist reactionary deviationists to the south – that would be China. The general said – 'wear something skyimpy'.

She was on fire that night, denouncing false paradigms and bourgeois modernity – but her audience, five hundred young soldiers in the dark, seemed distracted. Strange noises echoed in the wood and a heavy smell crept up to her on the warm night air. Like soup. Borscht. Fish borscht. And just as she was thinking this, the generator failed with a deep sigh and the stage lights went out and she was plunged into a pungent salty darkness ... being the plucky young pioneer that she was my Mother took out her torch and she switched it on and she saw them ... five hundred soldiers ... masturbating. Five hundred pale young faces ... a thousand eyes yellowed from the lack of vitamin D, heroes of the Soviet Union ... their hands a blur. And five hundred purple flowers startled by the sunlight – saluting.

So my point is this. Alex Syalmond, Annabel Gyoldie, Tavish Scyott you can call to us about our best and deepest instincts of compassion, justice and hope but what does it matter – deep down, you know yourselves –

the elecorate – we're all just a bunch of wankers. Welcome to the Hotel Caledonia. Soon my fellow worker Gavin will come in. Although he is a young Scottish man he also smells of fish borscht and whenever I see him – somehow I'm reminded of Kamchatka. Gavin!

**Gavin** Svetlana. Hi, I was just ... I hope you don't ... I just thought I'd ... Say hello.

**Svetlana** Gavin, I have just come on shift. It seems very busy. I see there is an event in the Tunnocks Tea Cake Ballroom. Are your people celebrating their proud decade of democratic enfranchisement and their hope for voting reform on this election day?

**Gavin** Eh ... no ... it's a weddin'.

**Svetlana** And who are the rest of the guests?

**Gavin** A couple of traveling salesmen. The Barr's Irn Bru Bar is full of writers – don't know who they are – they just turned up looking exhaust-ed, drunk and disappointed, and there's a man in the Macaroon Lounge who's a bit weird, can't look anybody in the eye. Anyway – the manager's worried we don't have enough custom. It's coming on to the height of the season and the bookings are low. People aren't spending their money. He's anxious.

**Svetlana** Let him sweat, it's what he's good at. I don't care about money.

**Gavin** You should care. Our jobs depend on people wanting to visit the Hotel Caledonia – that's what the manager says.

**Svetlana** The Hotel Caledonia is doomed Gavin. The management is hopeless. The staff are ill-educated and lazy. The rooms stink. Have you read TripAdvisor? Terry Waite, 'I missed my home comforts – even if I was chained to it, at least in Beirut there *was* a radiator.' No, the people and the infrastructure are hopeless Gavin. The only thing this place is good for is golf. Soon it will be a playground for American reactionaries in pastel coloured menswear.

**Gavin** That's terrible Svetlana ... what will happen to us?

**Svetlana** It doesn't bother me. I'm going home.

**Gavin** What?

**Svetlana** If I have to work in a terrible hotel for bad wages – at least I can do it in a place where I can express my contempt for my colleagues in my own language.

**Gavin**  But but –

**Svetlana**  But what Gavin?

**Gavin**  Svetlana – you can't leave.

**Svetlana**  Why not?

**Gavin**  Because … because …

**Svetlana**  What is it Gavin?

**Gavin**  Scotland is nice.

**Svetlana**  Elucidate.

**Gavin**  The scenery.

**Svetlana**  A tatty backdrop of faux romantic sublime created by ethnic cleansing and masquerading as wilderness.

**Gavin**  Castles.

**Svetlana**  Historical mythmaking and lickspittle toadying to a class structure of oppression and despair.

**Gavin**  And … ehmm … ehmmm … The people are friendly.

*The Manager shouts, offstage*

**Manager**  Ho! Svetty Betty. Get your arse in gear doll and bring the lads some lager would you. They're dying of thirst in the Caramel Log Suite. Gavin – there's twenty four trays of Buckfast and Tablet sorbet to be taken into the wedding breakfast. MOVE!

**Svetlana**  Buckfast and Tablet?

**Gavin**  Chef's been watching Heston Blumenthal. What are you doing?

**Svetlana**  I am googling, Gavin. I am googling Ryanair.

**Gavin**  Highland cows!

**Svetlana**  What about them.

**Gavin**  Hairy. Lovely eyes. Big eyes.

**Svetlana**  Hello is that Stansted Airport?

**Gavin**  No! Please. Svetlana. There must be something that would persuade you to stay?

**Svetlana**  Well, there is one thing. In Stansted Airport, I once had an epiphany. My flight from Vilnius got in at ten past midnight ... my flight to Prestwick was at seven in the morning. So I had to spend the night in the airport. I could not afford a hotel ... I thought there would be no one there but there were thousands of us. Thousands. The shops were shut. There was nowhere for us to sleep ... the chairs had been specially designed so that only a basketball player could lie down between them ... they had metal arms so you could not stretch out across them. Security personnel threatened anyone who lay down on the floor ... The night was hell.

But then dawn came – the gates were opened, and we thousand weary people checked in and went through security ... now the shops were open ... it was five in the morning, we were cold and hungry ... but all around us there were boutiques and perfumeries, coffee shops and restaurants ... and sweet, soothing music. We were human again. Three hours earlier we had been worthless, but not now. Now they had given us back our humanity. So long as we were spending, and money was passing through us, circulating like water in a pipe ... we were valued. We were customers. When money could not pass through us, we were shit.

I am not shit, Gavin, I don't want to be shit in a pipe. I don't want to be rich or poor. I want to be human. Show me that in Scotland I am not shit, Gavin. Tell me a story that I believe. Then maybe I will stay.

**Gavin**  Svetlana.

**Svetlana**  Yes.

**Gavin**  That is SO what I am going to do.

**Svetlana**  Good luck Gavin. You have 'til the poll's close.

*Svetlana tings the reception bell.*

**All**  (*singing*)
Plenty of room at the Hotel Caledonia.
Any time of year.
You can find us here.

## SCENE 2
### Svetlana and the Manager

*The McCowans Highland Chew Breakfast Pavillion. Svetlana is cleaning up dishes.*

**Manager**  Yo Svetlana – I've got a proposition for you. Sales are down. We need to sell ourselves. I'm doing a brochure and I want to put your face – *(stares at her chest)* – on it.

**Svetlana**  My face.

**Manager**  Face – and a certain amount of the area around your face. *(Stares at her chest.)* I would ask Catriona, but, between you and me, she's a bit too uptight ... and too chunky ... too ruddy cheeked, if you know what I mean. I thought your ... authentic Scottish features might sex it up a bit.

**Svetlana**  Scottish?

**Manager**  I also think your sweet, gentle curves would complement the lush undulating backdrop of Perthshire's finest hills.

**Svetlana**  What are you talking about?

**Manager**  Oh, don't worry. We won't have you prancing about the hills, Photoshop will take care of the scenery.

**Svetlana**  I'm not Scottish.

**Manager**  You don't need to be so literal Svetlana. You could be Scottish. Your Scottish-ness will be implied by everything else in the brochure. It's just a head shot, honestly. And a bit of cleavage. Fruity.

**Svetlana**  Fruity?

**Manager**  Soft fruit! Raspberries. The Perthshire raspberry end of things ... not ... you know ... kumquats or anything of that nature.

**Svetlana**  Can I think about it?

**Manager**  Sure. Go ahead. *(Stares at her. Long pause.)* Oh, you mean, actually think about it?

**Svetlana**  Yes.

**Manager**  What is there to think about. You're a loose spirit ... free.

**Svetlana**  You think I'm loose?

**Manager** I meant relaxed. Aren't you relaxed Svetlana. I thought you'd be one of them New Feminist thingys. You know, getting into all that burlesque malarky, and knitting in the park with no knickers on, and girl-on-girl tea parties. All that empowering stuff. I'll make it worth your while.

**Svetlana** No.

**Manager** Well, you don't have to answer this minute.

**Svetlana** My answer's no.

**Manager** The future of this hotel relies on a sexy advertising campaign. Just you have a wee think.

*Svetlana tings the reception bell.*

## SCENE 3
## STORIES FROM THE BAR FULL OF DRUNK AND EXHAUSTED WRITERS, VOL. 1

**Writer 1** Election time again. I leave my empathy at the polling station door. I hear myself saying the same old shit. Party A has pledged to do B and that would be good for me. Party C has pledged to do D and that's not going to benefit me. I wish 'me' wasn't the centre of my world. I wish I would think about the bigger picture. But it's the culture I suppose. I must climb the property ladder. I must look down on the 'scroungers', as they only have themselves to blame. I must lie and cheat to get my children into the best schools. I must complain that I pay too much tax; I don't even use the NHS. If I'm okay then everything is right with the world. Am I comfortable? Yes. I'm comfortable with mass unemployment, child poverty, scarce affordable housing, and a rising sexual crime rate. I think I'm trying to say I wish I had more of a social conscience. And I wish I would think before spending thousands on items of status or, say, £12 million on a car, like Chris Evans did. Can nothing better be done with this money? Are there no diseases in Africa? Are there no landmines in Cambodia? Do all of the world's children have access to clean water? I am defined by the choices I make. I am defined by how I treat others, especially those who have fewer choices than me. I am my internet history. I am the comments I post in anonymity. I am the money I have. I am the cars I drive. I am the boxes I cross on May 5th.

It should be simple, really. I imagine that one day I will be able to see beauty in the differences, not fear or disgust. I won't reduce people to one word; SLUT, FAT, PAKI, JUNKIE, FAG. I will realise that humans are more complex than that. In the future I will make bringing the cycles of neglect and abuse to an end a priority. It'll be expensive; I may have to empty my piggy bank. And I know I won't be alive to see the benefits but it'll be worth it. And they will be happy. And they will be smiling. And they will be dancing in the fields with tambourines and incense ... och, fuck it, I'm never going to be a great visionary or a great communicator, so, at the very least, can I put my energy into supporting those who are?

*Svetlana tings the tingy bell.*

**All**
The lads dance at the ceilidh
Smell of stale fags and sweat
Some dance to remember
Some dance to forget.

Ally Macleod was the Captain
I said bring me some wine.
He said we haven't had any spirit here
Since 1979.

And still those voices are calling from far far away
Wake me up in the middle of the night
Just to hear them say.

# SCENE 4
# A WOMAN IN WHITE

*A woman in white walks through the corridors.*

**Woman**  We are all ghosts here.

Don't think we're not. You can feel us and you can hear us. Turn up the heat. Turn up the volume. You can't quite obliterate our presence. We're ... lurking. That's what disembodied spirits do best. Lurk.

We lurk in damp grave clothes full of reproach.

We whisper in languages you no longer speak.

We smell of iron and steel and oil and engines you no longer make.

Our hands are raw from gutting herring and cod that no longer glitter in your sea.

Our feet are red and worn from tramping roads you speed down four abreast in foreign cars complaining about the state of the tarmac.

And we whisper ... all that work, all that work, what was it for ... what are you doing now with all the sweat we gave you. What was it all for?

*Svetlana tings the tingy bell.*

# SCENE 5
## THE MACKIE'S HONEYCOMB ICE CREAM PENTHOUSE

**Manager** (*clicks fingers*) Hey no slouching at reception, Svetty, wedding party's on its way.

**Svetlana** (*sighs, stands up straight*) Worry not, I will make the big effort for the happy couple.

**Manager** Well, you're half-right. They're a couple.

**Svetlana** But they are marrying today.

**Manager** A legal union will be taking place, yes.

**Svetlana** So why would they not be happy?

**Manager** Well. Her family's posh and his aren't, and that kinday thing in Scotland? Let's just say there's a reason Cinderella's a fairy tale.

**Svetlana** But they must be in love, no?

**Manager** It gets worse. He's ... (*kicks with his right foot*) and she's ... (*kicks with left foot*).

**Svetlana** They are footballers?

**Manager** He's a hun and she's a tim.

**Svetlana** Ah, this is good! These are good reasons to stay in Scotland!

**Manager** What are?

**Svetlana** Two footballers! The one who is the hunk but poor is marrying his boyfriend Tim who is rich. This could not happen in my country!

**Manager**  Naw, listen. It's no two men. He's Protestant and she's Catholic.

**Svetlana**  Oh, I see. And that is dangerous?

**Manager**  It is if you're Neil Lennon. Man's probably feart to open an email attachment.

**Svetlana**  But I thought Scotland hated England?

**Manager**  Aye they do, but that's just a pastime. Scots save their *real* venom for other Scots.

**Svetlana**  Explain.

**Manager**  Right, well, the Huns hate the Tims and the Tims hate the Huns. The Highlands hate Glasgow and Glasgow hates –

**Svetlana**  The Highlands?

**Manager**  Edinburgh.

**Svetlana**  Does Edinburgh hate Glasgow?

**Manager**  Naw, Edinburgh hates tourists. The Scots who stay hate the Scots who leave. The Scots who leave hate the Scots who stay. Scottish Scots hate the wans who sound English. Anglo Scots hate the wans who sound Scottish. Which is why there's likely to be trouble between the McFuckwits and the Medley-Warners through there. Posh bastards.

**Svetlana**  This is more complicated than I thought.

**Manager**  Ye'll get the hangay it. Let's try a wee test. What school did you go to?

**Svetlana**  Saint Peter's.

**Manager**  So you were home-educated! How interesting.

**Svetlana**  No, I said –

**Manager**  What football team do you support?

**Svetlana**  Moscow Dynamo.

**Manager**  Ah, Partick Thistle! They're doing well in the league. What do you think of Scotland's chances in the World Cup?

**Svetlana**  Shit.

**Manager**  Correct. You'll be fine. (*Exits.*)

**Svetlana**  How many times can you fold a piece of paper?

You know, in Russia they found the most hated man in country. He is not a dictator. Or murderer. He is a gardener.

For comedy show in Russia they do sketch. They ask Russians: what is worst place in all of country? Russians say: 'Ah it is Moscow. They are arrogant, they are aloof, they do not care for their fellow human.'

So they go to Moscow and they ask people on street, 'What is worst place in all of Moscow?' And they say, 'It is Vorksplek! It is dangerous place, no walk there at night someone will stab you.'

And they go to Vorksplek and they say, 'What is worst place in whole of Vorksplek?' And the people say, 'There is street here, where all the young people they stand at night and they are swearing, and the gardens they are mess. And there is the dogs faeces all over the place. And the families, they very bad.'

And they go to this street and they say, 'Which is worst house in this street?' And the people say, 'The man at the end of the street, he is always gardening, but really he is watching what we are doing all the time.'

And they go to this man's house and he is in his garden tending his flowers and they say, 'Did you know you are most hated man in Russia?'

And he stands up and he says, 'No.'

And they say 'Who do you hate?'

And he says, 'I don't hate anyone. But if you don't get out of my garden I will call the police.'

It is not just Scotland. It is everywhere. So what would be the point of going home?

# SCENE 6
## STORIES FROM THE BAR FULL OF DRUNK AND EXHAUSTED WRITERS, VOL 2.

**Writer 2**  Sorry, this wasn't what I was supposed to write but a lot's happened recently.

Cameron was on the Today programme today. He accepted he'd failed to get rid of Punch and Judy politics. No, he didn't accept it, he boasted about it. 'I think I've already told you, on this very programme, that I've failed to get rid of Punch and Judy politics.' He crowed. No-one, possibly no-one ever, crows like Cameron.

Punch and Judy politics. In the last week we, and I don't mean we, I mean you, Cameron, tried to kill a man. But you're no commander-in-chief. You're Obama-lite. You were so jealous on Monday watching the crowds in Times Square. They shot a man in the eye and Geronimo. Everyone loves the president.

But when you went for Gaddafi, you missed your target. Just killed his son and three grandchildren. His son, by some unwritten rule, now has to be referred to as his 'playboy son'. So that's alright then. The grand-kids ... collateral damage. It's Gaddafi's fault. After 1986, when Thatcher let Reagan bomb Libya from British bases, we killed two of his sons then. When will he learn. Be nice, trade fairly, your sons live. Fuck us around and we'll kill your family. I say us, I mean you.

But it's a Scottish election tonight. What's to be done? None of this is devolved. Frankly, from Thatcher to Cameron, with warmonger Blair there for most of the intervening, it's not even undevolved. No major political party has stood up to the challenge. Robin Cook wanted an ethical foreign policy, but found it difficult. Of course it's difficult. That's why we have elections. To choose people to do difficult things.

Which brings me to the point. I wanted to try and find one thing about Scottish politics that I could stand and applaud. Not just tolerate, but get into arguments defending. Marcus Aurelius said that 'the best revenge is to be unlike him who performed the injury'. I'm ashamed to be British after last week. But I'm slightly proud to have a vote in the Scottish Elections when in the last term our government followed the rule of law rather than an instinct for vengeance, and released Abdelbaset Mohmed Ali al-Megrahi on compassionate grounds. I would be even prouder if I didn't feel that both the politicians and the people of Scotland regretted he wasn't dead by now. A warning Megrahi, continue to live and we'll send Cameron after your kids.

## SCENE 7
## THE CHOCOLATE AND VANILLA SLIDER
## BUSINESS CENTRE

*Svetlana is laying out sandwiches for a corporate event.*

**Boy** Here, wifie, can I interest you in purchasing a fine work of artwork?

**Svetlana** Who are you – how did you get in here?

**Boy** I have a technique.

**Svetlana** What?

**Boy** Read it in a book. Look like you belong. Nobody'll ever stop ye. So I walked in here like I owned the joint. Bingo. Also – your security guy's asleep. Anyway – I'm selling art here – you interested?

**Svetlana** An artwork? Let's see? (*Boy holds up the picture*) Oh god, no way.

**Boy** Fifty quid.

**Svetlana** No thank you.

**Boy** Fifteen quid.

**Svetlana** No.

**Boy** You're getting the frame for free.

**Svetlana** No thanks.

**Boy** Fifteen quid, it's a bargain.

**Svetlana** That picture is disgusting and degrading to women.

**Boy** What?

**Svetlana** It's a pornographic picture and it doesn't even have a head.

**Boy** I could get you a head.

**Svetlana** No.

*He's about to walk off.*

**Boy** Help me oot here lady. I need to pay my electricity meter.

**Svetlana** How much is it.

**Boy** Fifteen pound. See, my mum geid me a tenner tae top up the meter card. But, I'm smart see. There's fifteen on the meter so we're five short so I took the tenner doon the market and bought this fancy frame and put this artistic nude poster fae my bedroom wall in it. I reckon I can sell it for fifteen.

**Svetlana** Artistic nude? The poster's got a hole where her fanny is.

**Boy** Gies it character though.

**Svetlana** It has a certain cubist charm.

**Boy** How much do you think I should insure it for?

**Svetlana** You must know somebody who can lend you fifteen pounds.

**Boy** I dinnae want a lend. I'm nae intae loaning anymair. I've had enough o' the sharks threatening me with the old anal rape. I'm making my own way in the world. I'm standing on my oan two feet. I'm an entrepreneur. Hey, do you think any o' them old men in suits dancing like fuds wid want tae buy it?

**Svetlana** You're not going in there. It's a wedding and I don't think they want you touting porn about the place.

**Boy** Come on, look this place is dead boring. Put this baby on the wall. Liven the place up.

**Svetlana** It doesn't need livening up.

**Boy** Wifie! I'm desperate here. Give me a chance will you?

**Svetlana** Look – it's election day. Your situation as a proletarian is desperate but surely one of the parties has a policy aimed at guiding you and your class towards a more secure future. Vote for them. This is better than touting pornography.

**Boy** I'm sorry I just didnae understand a single thing you said there.

**Svetlana** WHY DON'T YOU VOTE?

**Boy** I wid if they gied me fifteen quid, like. I need tae make some money, wifie.

**Svetlana** Politics – that's the way to make a change – not these small individualistic gestures towards self improvement. Class struggle for class progress.

**Boy** Politics though. They all look like fuds. They all sound like fuds. Ken, politics tae me is just one giant fud. My heid gets lost in it.

**Svetlana** Then the capitalistic class has won! First you gain consciousness of your true situation. Then you fight. Then you spread the word. You win some battles, you lose some battles but as long as they were worth fighting for you will be on the side of history. You've got an hour left to vote. Vote.

**Boy** I've got an hour tae top up the meter card afore Scotmid shuts and I'm still fifteen quid short.

**Svetlana** I'll give you fifteen pounds. (*Taking money out of pocket.*) As long as you promise to vote.

**Boy** I cannae take it –

**Svetlana** Please

**Boy** Take this (*holding up the picture*).

**Svetlana** Oh-god-what-am-I-doing. Deal.

**Boy** (*They swap money for picture.*) Fucking ace.

**Svetlana** Promise.

**Boy** Promise.

**Svetlana** I think I did a good thing for Scotland there.

*She tings the bell.*

# SCENE 8
## THE WEE JIMMY KRANKIE EXECUTIVE BAR AND LOUNGE

**Svetlana** Yes sir, what can I do for you?

**Wedding Guest** I'm not sure yet ... I'm considering alternatives.

**Svetlana** Alternatives?

**Wedding Guest** Who I want to shag – order of tactical preference.

**Svetlana** I see.

**Wedding Guest** I don't know if you do ... it's a whole new approach I'm trying. See, I really like the look of you, but there's that Australian wait-ress ... and there's Claire of course.

**Svetlana** Claire?

**Wedding Guest** The bridesmaid ... I used to go with her before, but now? And she's the bridesmaid ... I mean, I'd like to avoid clichés if possible.

**Svetlana** You Scots. You are very romantic.

**Wedding Guest** You are my first choice. But I quite like that waitress. The Australian. Or Claire.

**Svetlana** You should go for Claire.

**Wedding Guest** Not the Australian?

**Svetlana** No, Claire. You know her name.

**Wedding Guest** Hmmm ... but I already *know* what Claire's like, and I like a new challenge. Besides, if you stick to one choice you might end up stuck for life.

**Svetlana** Or she might not be available.

**Wedding Guest** Yeah, and I might get stuck with somebody my family or my mates choose for me ...

**Svetlana** You should go for what you want. What you really really want.

**Wedding Guest** Shall I tell you what I want? What I really really want?

**Svetlana** Uncommited, amoral fornication?

**Wedding Guest** See we call that 'shagging'. There's so much I could teach you. Fuck it ... I'm going for all three of you. Law of averages says I'm bound to end up with one of you.

**Svetlana** I do not want your future ... and I am indifferent to your past. For selfish reasons, even though I do not approve, I must now ask you to harass the Australian or the bridesmaid.

**Wedding Guest** Second or third choice, but they needn't know that. See, the beauty of this alternative vote system is there is always a fifty-one per-cent chance of getting my tick in somebody's box. Under the previous first past the post system, more than likely I'd end up walking home electorally unsatisfied.

**Svetlana** Well that is this voting round over. NEXT!

*She tings the bell.*

**All**
Mould on most of the ceilings
At night my airse feels like ice
When I complain the receptionist says
What did you expect at this reasonable price.

And in the cold business centre
The rich men have their needs
They have a seamstress in Bangalore
To knit their personal tweeds.

*Svetlana tings the tingy bell.*

**Svetlana** Next!

# SCENE 9
# IN THE GLEN MICHAEL AND PALADIN MEMORIAL GARDEN

*Night. A couple hurry away from the wedding.*

**Woman**  Get through here. There's no enough room on that flair.

**Man**  My word, that was lively! Someone's spilled red wine all over my shirt!

**Woman**  Naw, it's blood.

**Man**  What?

**Woman**  Dinnay worry, I don't think it's yours. Just call it a welcome from Scotland.

**Man**  It's *very* different to an English wedding, isn't it?

**Woman**  Aye, ye cannay dance like that on horseback.

**Man**  I see what people mean now about the cultural differences.

**Woman**  Thought you woulda been useday that.

**Man**  How so?

**Woman**  Well, were you no pals at universisty wi Whitsherface?

**Man**  Fiona. The bride.

**Woman**  Aye, her. Sorry, I keep forgetting.

**Man**  Not really much of a bridesmaid are you?

**Woman**  Hoy, cheeky, I'm an amazing bridesmaid. (*Does a twirl.*) Just no keen on Whitsherface.

**Man**  Fiona.

**Woman**  Uptay ma brither if *he* wants tay marry her. But for me she's too fwah fwah fwah.

**Man**  You don't like posh accents?

**Woman**  No on a woman, no.

**Man**  But on a man?

**Woman**  On a man it's quite sexy. (*Lusty glance.*)

**Man**  Indeed. So that dance? What's it called.

**Woman**  Canadian Barn Dance, sweetheart. We used to get it in school every Christmas.

**Man**  Some sort of native tradition?

**Woman**  Naw, mair like child abuse. Boys line up one side of the gym hall, girls line up the other. Look I'll show ye. Staun there.

**Man**  Um, okay.

**Woman**  Pretend ye're thirteen. And ye're from Glasgow.

**Man**  Um … used any good … *blades* … lately?

**Woman**  Hands in yer pockets, chew yer gum, and lie tay yer pal about the things ye've done wi us.

**Man**  See that redhead over there? She told me a rude joke.

**Woman**  You've totally never shagged.

**Man**  Of course not, I'm thirteen!

**Woman**  Okay gentleman's choice. Select your partner for the Canadian Barn Dance! Now walk towards me, kidding on that this is a total drag.

**Man**  Ugh! This is a total drag.

**Woman**  Don't walk too fast or people will know that ye're goin for me and ye'll get the pish ripped out of ye.

**Man**  Sounds painful.

**Woman**  It is. Walk too slow but, and sumday else will get me.

**Man**  Can't have that.

**Woman**  I'm a prize alright.

**Man**  The jewel of the crown.

**Woman**  Awright, whit ye wantin?

**Man**  Oh, we're acting now, I see.

**Woman**  In Glasgow we're always acting. Whit ye wantin?

**Man**  Hello. I was wondering if you'd oblige me in a dance this evening?

**Woman**  Whit? I cannay understaun whit ye're sayin.

**Man**  Wid ye. Like ti. Haya wee JIG. Wammay mi?

**Woman**  Naw, you're supposed tay say: Ye dancin?

**Man**  Ye dancin?

**Woman**  Ye askin?

**Man**  Ye askin?

**Woman**  That's *ma* line. It's all partay the courtship ritual, ye see. We're very particular about wur totty up here. So ye havetay go through the correct exchange.

**Man**  My word, it's like Brideshead Revisited.

**Woman**  Well I'm no the bride, I'll no be givin ye head. And we'll certainly no be revisitin it if ye dinnay ask a lady tay dance in a manner appropriate tay wur country, OKAY?

**Man**  Okay!

**Woman**  You say: I'm askin.

**Man**  (*clears throat, opens arms*) I'm askin!

**Woman**  I'm dancin.

**Man**  Excellent.

**Woman**  But watch cos I go fast. Take my haun here.

**Man**  Right.

**Woman**  And haud ma waist there. Ready?

**Man**  Uh.

**Woman**  Heel toe. Heel. Toe. Et cetera, et cetera. (*She teaches him the Canadian Barn Dance.*) Och, you're rubbish at this.

**Man**  Slow down then!

**Woman**  I did warn ye. Scream if you wanna go faster!

(*Laughter. She birls him. He stops her, holds her firmly.*)

**Woman**  Hey, the dance isnay finished.

**Man**  I'm going to kiss you.

**Woman**  Whit for?

**Man** So you'll kiss me back.

**Woman** I cannay dae that.

**Man** Why not?

**Woman** 'Cos I'm a bridesmaid. I have tay set an example.

**Man** You could always make it a *bad* example ... I've seen you looking at me all night, you little Scottish pop-tart.

**Woman** We shouldnay. We're both married.

**Man** Happily married?

**Woman** *(sigh)* Wha is? But a union's for keeps, is it no? For better or worse.

**Man** Look, if there's one thing that Margaret Thatcher taught us. It's that unions just get in the way. Ha ha.

**Woman** Whit?

**Man** Come on, just one kiss.

**Woman** *(steps back)* Here, you're no a Tory, are ye?

**Man** Do you really want to get into this? Come on, it's a wedding. Politics doesnay really suit the mood.

**Woman** Kinday hard tay avoid the day, pal *(points to TV)*.

**Man** In which case ... She did have *some* good policies, you know.

**Woman** Policies? Up here, she reduced them doontay just wan: a scorched earth policy. Why do ye think Scotland's the wey it is noo?

**Man** Excuse me, what about New Labour? Devolution? Thatcher was a long time ago, get over it.

**Woman** Aye, well you brought her up, pal! It might've been a long time ago, but ye might've noticed there's a recession on. We're still *living* it.

**Man** C'mon, this door's open, let's go in here.

**Woman** Naw. Stop. Look, I do fancy ye, right.

**Man** I know you do.

**Woman** I mean, I *like* a bastard. Just no a Tory bastard.

**Man** Well excuse me.

**Woman** And don't get me wrong, sometimes an ordinary Scottish lassie like me does get Tory-curious. But it's an election day in Scotland, pal. I canny snog wannay youse on an *election day*. It'd be sacrilegious. Be like fartin at Mass.

**Man** I only said she had some good policies. I never said I was Tory.

**Woman** Aye, but ye are though eh? Can tell just by looking at you.

**Man** Maybe I voted Lib Dem.

**Woman** So I was right then.

**Man** Okay, so what if I was a Tory? Would that stop us being attracted to each other?

**Woman** Em, do cats fancy dugs?

**Man** Oh, I'm sorry. There was me looking *forward* to coming to Scotland because of the friendliness of your people, your welcoming character, I didn't realise you practice such a selective discrimination.

**Woman** Oh it's no selective. We hate everybody. Just hate youse maist.

**Man** Oh and who would you prefer? A racist party like the SNP.

**Woman** Racist?

**Man** Yes, a country whose only purpose is to demonise the English as the source of all of Scotland's problems.

**Woman** Well okay, I mean, yese *never* forced George Galloway ontay Big Brother, but –

**Man** You know what's wrong with Scotland?

**Woman** Em, let me see. Oil revenue? The democratic defecit? That we're always the bridesmaid and never the bride?

**Man** No, I'll tell you Scotland's problem. You're holding it in your hand right now.

**Woman** Ah. The demon drink. (*She throws it in his face.*) Problem solved.

*Svetlana tings the tingy bell.*

# SCENE 10
# SVETLANA & THE PHOTOGRAPHER

*Night. The Scrooge McDuck Lounge Bar and Snug. Svetlana is cleaning glasses. Gavin is leaning against the bar and the Manager enters with a camera in a state of barely suppressed excitement.*

**Manager**  I got the camera.

**Svetlana**  I told you I didn't want to pose for photos.

**Manager**  It's a' right darling. I'll be gentle. It's just a head shot. One click and it's all over.

**Svetlana**  Please, Gavin …

**Manager**  Listen Svetty, I've heard whispers that you're thinking of leaving us. If you're looking for another job you'll need a reference, won't you? Who do you think writes that reference?

**Svetlana**  Exploiting dog.

**Manager**  That's my girl. Alrighty. If you'd like tae stand next tae the table o' Scottish paraphernalia.

**Svetlana**  Here?

**Manager**  That's good, aye. Noo, say 'hoots mon' for the camera.

**Svetlana**  Hoots mon?

**Manager**  Hooots mon.

**Svetlana**  Hoooots mon.

**Manager**  That's it. Really pucker up for the hooo.

**Svetlana**  Hoooo. Is that it finished?

**Manager**  I'm actually just warming the camera up darling. I've nae taken the actual shot yet. Hoots mon.

**Svetlana**  Hoots mon.

**Manager**  Hands on your hips, chest forward, lips oot. Hooots mon.

**Svetlana**  Hooots mon.

**Manager**  Can we get the tartan sash roond you. Aye, and I'm getting a lot o' glare fae the windae. You'll have tae bend ower a bitty.

**Svetlana**  Like this?

**Manager**  Marvellous quine. Marvellous. I didnae realise how nice your shoes are. Could we get a foot up on the table. And lean the rest o' your body back. Oh, yes. Hoots mon.

**Svetlana**  Hoots mon.

**Manager**  Hoo aboot a fling?

**Svetlana**  A what?

**Manager**  A highland fling. Gavin, show her. (*Gavin strikes a pose, Svetlana copies.*) And hold it …

**Svetlana**  This

**Manager**  You widnae

**Svetlana**  Is

**Manager**  Even

**Svetlana**  Fucking

**Manager**  Ken you're

**Svetlana**  Awful.

**Manager**  Latvian.

**Svetlana**  I'm Lithuanian!

**Manager**  Noo pour some whisky. Bend ower, lower your chest, pour some whisky. Look tae the camera. Noo wi a smile. Noo wi a hoots mon.

**Svetlana**  Hoots mon.

**Manager**  Open a few buttons o your shirt noo. Dinnae be shy. Come on, liberate your Paps of glencoe.

*Svetlana is starting to back away and not participate, the Manager hardly notices as he's getting carried away.*

Pick up the haggis. Oh aye, caress the haggis. Oh aye, run your fingers all ower the haggis. Spank it. Spank the haggis. Spank it hard. Spank the haggis. Lick it. Spank it. Lick it. Spank it. Oh god. I'm done.

**Svetlana**  That's it, that's enough.

**Manager** But we didn't get the picture I wanted. I need one of you playing the chanter.

**Svetlana** You can stick your chanter, and stick your photos, and stick your reference up your –

**Manager** There, got it – perfect. That's just what I needed – passion!

*Svetlana tings the tingy bell.*


# SCENE 11
# THE MCEWAN'S GROUSEBEATER MEMORIAL MEZZANINE

*The Mother and Father of the groom drink.*

**Mother** He's not my son anymore. I've lost him for socialism.

**Father** Don't say that.

**Mother** He's not.

**Father** You don't mean that.

**Mother** I do.

**Father** It's the Chardonnay talking, you should have stopped at the toasts.

**Mother** I don't know who he is any more.

**Father** But you like Fiona. You like her. You can't blame the girl.

**Mother** Fiona? Why would I blame Fiona?

**Father** You wanted them to get married.

**Mother** I'm delighted they got married, I'm not blaming Fiona for anything. I'm blaming you.

**Father** Me?

**Mother** You.

**Father** For what!?

**Mother** Know what he told me? He's not going to vote. Doesn't see the point.

**Father** And that's *my* fault?

**Mother** He was a boy who cared about everything, *everything*. He would pick an earthworm out of a puddle so it wouldn't drown. He'd stand up to the teachers if another kid got a telling off. And now he doesn't care enough to vote?

**Father** Did you have those hot whisky cocktails?

**Mother** You're not listening to me.

**Father** I am listening to you, and I suspect a lethal combo of grain and grape.

**Mother** You can make a speech about anything except something that really matters. What happened to the man who ran with me on the streets shouting about the poll tax?

**Father** Mary, if we were all still running on the streets...

**Mother** You cared about everything then too...

**Father** And what good did it do us!?

**Mother** *There* you go!

**Father** What?

**Mother** That's the death of our son's political conscience right there. We had a baby who thought he could be part of the world and now we've got a man who thinks there's no point trying to be part of anything but your local gym.

**Father** At least he's fit. And anyway, what about you? What's your part in the death of our baby's youthful idealism? Or are you blameless?

**Mother** I said nothing. I watched and I said nothing. I'm worse than you.

**Father** Aw Jesus, don't cry, seriously Mary, don't...

**Mother** We've ruined him!

**Father** Did you have liqueurs as well?

**Mother** (*snuffling*) A wee Baileys.

**Father** Please Mary, don't sing, promise me...

**Mother** I thought it would all come right in the end. I thought, 'What can you do? Running in the streets doesn't work, just sit tight, stay quiet, look after your gorgeous wee boy and he'll fix the world for all of us, how could he not? He was such a caring wee soul ... And because I never spoke up ... because I never spoke up he doesn't even care enough to vote!

I says to him, I says 'I hope you got your postal vote booked before the honeymoon,' and he just laughed! He laughed. 'Och no, we forgot, never mind, if voting changed anything they'd make it illegal eh?' And I couldny say anything after that because Fiona was tossing the bouquet and it all went wrong and hit your Auntie Helen in the face and now her contacts are on the floor and she can't see to find her car keys ... which is just as well because she had the hot whisky cocktail too.

**Father** I'll just go and get you a coffee.

**Mother** *Don't leave me!*

**Father** Mary.

**Mother** Socialism's dead and my boy's off to Fuertaventura and he's never coming home again. What have I got left? What have I got left to fight for?

*He takes her hand. They sit a moment, Mother starts to nod, listening to an inaudible beat. Then, abruptly, she starts to sing. She's singing, 'Ghost Town' by The Specials.*

**Mother** This town ... is coming like a ghost town ...

**Father** Oh for the love of god.

*Svetlana tings the tingy bell.*

# SCENE 12
# WOMAN IN WHITE

*A woman in white walks through the corridors.*

**Woman** I walk down the corridors of this place. They're endless. I listen at the door of every room. I hear arguments. I hear noisy sex. I hear quiet sex too because I keep my ear pressed to the door until I've heard something. I hear people taking the complimentary toiletries and wondering if its stealing. I hear people taking the bedspreads, the sheets, the bathroom fittings and the light bulbs and calling it compensation for poor service. I hear the last breath of the guest who checked in for the last weekend break they'll ever know. I hear the first high choking sob of the unexpected daughter born to the terrified fifteen year old in room 4007, (she's here with her extended family for her Gran's seventieth birthday and she just thought she had bloating and indigestion). I hear drunken parties joyfully trashing the mini bar. I hear furtive diners eating brought in sandwiches under the covers because they can't afford the breakfast rate. The lights flicker as I walk. My feet stick to the unwashed carpet. I hear children crying. I hear women crying. I hear men crying. I hear as many of one as the other … I walk and I walk and I never see another guest. I stand in the middle of one of the endless corridors and I scream, 'This isn't good enough! Come out and talk to me! This isn't good enough!'. And behind all the millions of doors it all goes quiet … and not one door opens. They all wait, listening until I walk away.

*Svetlana tings the tingy bell.*

**All** (*singing*)
Last thing I remember
I was running for the door
I had to find the passage back
To the way I was before

Chill oot said reception
Don't be so naïve
You can check out any time you like
But you can never leave.

*Ting.*

# SCENE 13
## STORIES FROM THE BAR FULL OF DRUNK AND EXHUASTED WRITERS, VOL 3.

**Writer 3** I was born in 1975 and grew up on a new-build housing scheme in Falkirk filled mainly with new parents and their broods. Every house was identical and the 'fences' between the gardens were about a foot high, to encourage neighbourliness. Sure enough on a summer's day you could literally walk in and out of all the other gardens, and people did. There were parties every weekend and after every Scotland game. And there were children *everywhere*. Know that bit in *Gregory's Girl* when Gregory comes out of his house and has to navigate his way past about thirty toddlers? It was like that. As the eighties went on, though, people started buying their council houses. Now we all know the consequences in terms of a property market but my child's eye perspective was this: the fences got bigger.

Someone bought their house: they changed their front door, and built a fence. A fence was a clear sign to the neighbourhood that the person who lived behind it was a property-owner. Then someone else would buy their home and there was a bigger fence. People still spoke to each other from their gardens in the summer, just that now they were leaning on fences to do it. As the eighties became the nineties, the fences were too high for people to see over. The parties stopped. New neighbours came and went without people ever really knowing anything about them. We were all middle class now. And twenty years later if we've been lucky enough to avoid being made redundant we're working every hour god sends to pay our mortgage and our debt, coming home to crash, knackered, in front of the telly for two hours of brain decharging, going through a bottle of wine a night, wondering, if the worst comes to the worst could we cope with the *shame* of insolvency. The *reek* of it. And so we work. Let's face it, we're all working class now. We always were. So why can't we go back to the start. Pull the fences down. Let the toddlers out. Who wants to have a street party?

*Svetlana tings the tingy bell.*

# SCENE 14
## SVETLANA & THE SLOGAN

*The Dame Michelle Mone Wetroom Cum Conservatory. Svetlana polishes the leaves of the yucca plants.*

**Manager** Yo, Svet. Here it is. The finished product. Don't get too excited, this is just a prototype. But be assured there are hundreds of thousands of copies flying off the press, about to wing their way to Tourist Information, Edinburgh, London, New York, Fochabers. Ta-da! (*He produces a brochure.*)

**Svetlana** Oh my god. That's me! Why am I naked?

**Manager** It's brilliant.

**Svetlana** Wait, that's not ... my body. How could this happen? Wait a minute ... there's a hole in the fanny.

**Manager** Is there? Oh shit, we meant to photoshop Nessie coming out of there.

**Svetlana**  This is that boy's pornographic artwork. You've put my head on the top. Is this some kind of crazy, sick, revolting joke?

**Manager**  Why is it sick? I think it's a fairly traditional and accurate portrait of modern Scotland. Don't you think? I mean, there's the red squirrel nibbling on a piece of shortbread on your shoulder. We've got a piper in the background. A golf club in your hand …

**Svetlana**  It's not my hand!

**Manager**  … a ghost of a saltire in the clear blue sky. And do you like the quote?

**Svetlana**  Hotel Caledonia; The Best *Small* Hotel in the World –

**Manager**  Best *Small* Hotel in the World. Fantastic, ay?

**Svetlana**  Do you mean this place?

**Manager**  Indeed I do.

**Svetlana**  How do you know it's the best small hotel in the world?

**Manager**  What do you mean how do I know?

**Svetlana**  By what criteria? What evidence?

**Manager**  It just is.

**Svetlana**  Is it.

**Manager**  It's a quote.

**Svetlana**  A quote from who?

**Manager**  Me.

**Svetlana**  Right. And if you print enough of them it must be true.

**Manager**  It's the sort of thing people say. And why shouldn't we be the best. I believe that if we say we're the best then we ARE the best. We need to start talking ourselves up.

**Svetlana**  Everything about this leaflet is a lie. Do you think people are going to believe this? I'm not even Scottish.

**Manager**  Look Svetty – I have a hotel to fill. I could go serving up contemporary cuisine, and video game seminars and offering study tours of the deprived parts of Glasgow so we could represent something you might think of as the true picture of Scotland. Or I could say – fuck truth.

The truth doesn't sell hotel rooms.

**Svetlana** You cannot print this. I do not give you my permission to use my image.

**Manager** You should've read the small print in your contract.

**Svetlana** What contract?

**Manager** Exactly. Welcome to the Hotel Caledonia, Svetty.

**Svetlana** I hate this place. That's it, I'm going.

*Boy runs into hotel, he's clearly in a hurry and not stopping long.*

**Boy** Here, wifie, wifie

**Svetlana** You again?

**Boy** You're a fucking genius.

**Svetlana** And you're a pain in the neck

**Boy** How?

**Svetlana** Look what my Manager did with your picture.

**Boy** That. Is … beautiful.

**Svetlana** What do you want, boy.

**Boy** I came to tell you my exciting news.

**Svetlana** Did you vote?

**Boy** I did more than vote. I double voted. I voted times a thousand.

**Svetlana** Is this some comment on AV?

**Boy** Naw. Stupid. I wis telling my cousin Franny about whit you said aboot startin a movement, and then I had a fuckin marvellous brain wave. I thought – I need tae get my people organised. I need to exercise the same entrepreneurial attitude I've brought tae the electricity meter problem and bring that tae bear on liberating the underclass from the poverty problem.

**Svetlana** I'm encouraged to hear it –

**Boy** I thought, how can I bring about a revolution and make money at the same time?

**Svetlana** It's not orthodox Marxism but still –

**Boy** We're going tae make a fuckin fortune Wifie, you and me.

**Svetlana** Me?

**Boy** You're an investor.

**Svetlana** In what?

**Boy** If industrially processed you can decorate a pill for approximately one pence a unit. Fifteen quid equals 1,500 units. My cousin Franny had the pills. I came up with the design and here it is – one and a half thousand ecstasy tabs each one individually embossed wi a picture of a fanny and the words 'Vote Ya Cunts'.

**Svetlana** Please just keep the money. I'm not an investor.

**Boy** Suit yersel. I'm off tae sell these. This is the start of something really big. I can tell.

**Svetlana** It's a shame I won't be in Scotland to see it.

**Boy** I'm off tae encourage my comrades tae vote.

**Svetlana** Boy, you do know the election is finished, don't you.

**Boy** What? Is there not an election every day?

**Svetlana** It's over now.

**Boy** Shite.

**Svetlana** I'm sorry.

**Boy** Och, we'll just save them for the X Factor then.

*Ting.*

# SCENE 15
## STORIES FROM THE BAR FULL OF DRUNK AND EXHAUSTED WRITERS, VOL 4.

**Writer 4** Suppose they put up a wall? This was me talking to a pal of mine, another Scot in exile, I think it was about the time of the last election. We were talking about the SNP getting a majority in the Scottish Parliament and we said, 'Suppose they put up a wall?' And we're laughing but there's this tiny … fear's the wrong word … this awoken … instinct in his eyes. And we both know we're thinking exactly the same thing. If Scotland was going off anywhere, we'd have to run home before she left. Anything happens up here ... we'd need to get back. We'd always need to get home.

There you go. Home. Haven't had a home here for eighteen years.

I am the classic cliché. The weeping Scot in exile. Sinking Japanese whisky and weeping about glens I never walked. I look back at Scotland with sentiment, with nostalgia, through glasses tinted so deeply rosy pink its a wonder the whole nation doesn't look like a heap of candy floss.

Shall I tell you what that view's like?

When my Mum goes into the hospital in the Borders they're talking about the cuts, and God knows some pretty vital stuff is trembling on the verge of extinction in the health service ... but her wait is half an hour, not seven and the nurse that sees her remembers her name and what sport she watches on the television.

My friend's kid in Glasgow has got himself half way through uni and they can still afford a family holiday. I can't. Not in London. I've had to take out an extra mortgage to keep my son in education.

There's folk up here prepared to pay good money to come and see half written plays about the state of their nation. Down in London you struggle to fill a theatre with anything that doesn't have a Lloyd Webber tune attached.

And there's something else, I come up here, I come home, and people are still having the same arguments they were having eighteen years ago. Arguments about politics and parties and identity and ... Oh God that is *so* good. You've no idea how good that is ... because I'd nearly forgotten that anyone, anywhere thought there was any point in argument, any point in protest, any point in anything. In the cynical south there are only two truths left – everyone lies and nothing matters except looking after your own money.

Maybe you can't see it – maybe you're too close to it – maybe its being eroded so fast it's already doomed ... but there is still a community in Scotland. There are still community values, even if we never agree what they are. There is still ... hope.

Oh I know. The glasses are rosy, rosy pink but sometimes, when I come home, I almost want to say, 'Oh quick, build a wall, build a wall before those buggers come roaring up north and grab that hope off us and take it away for good.'

*Svetlana tings the tingy bell.*

# SCENE 16
# THE FATHER OF THE BRIDE

*The Tunnocks Teacake Banqueting Room*

**Dad**  I'm here to raise a toast ... to two young people ... my daughter Fiona ... and ... (*struggles to remember*) it'll come ... to ask you to raise your glasses to them ... and to the future.

I don't know if I can do that.

What changed? What changed? Three years ago ... I remember asking the bank manager ... what just changed? I mean ... when the ... financial crisis ... what was it that really changed? Did the world really suddenly get poorer? Why, all of a sudden ... was all the work we did ... not worth anything anymore ... why were we ...

**Bride**  Dad ...

**Dad**  And it's an election day ... election day ... that's supposed to be about the future anaw ... isn't it?

**Bride**  Dad ... just make the toast ...

**Dad**  The toast ... (*He suddenly decides to tell the truth. To Bride.*) Fuck it ... This is the one day ... Fiona ... this is the one day I've got left in my lying ... stupid life ... this is the last day I've got when you're all supposed to listen to me.

(*To audience.*) I want to toast their future. But I want to toast their REAL future ... but that's the fucking joke ... I don't know what's gonnae happen, do I?

But whatever the future is ... tonight ... tonight at least ... it's not going to begin with a lie ...

**Bride**  Dad ... I think that's enough

**Dad**  Shut your face, Fiona ... you didn't even vote ... and neither did you ... thingymy ... did ye? Did any of ye? Whatever happens today, let's not lie ... just because we're drinking champagne ...

(*Back to speech.*) Iain Gray ... he seems like a decent enough goob ... so what? Alec Salmond is a tricky wee fucker ... so what? It's not about them. It's us. Us here ...

We don't change our lives like we change our mortgage provider. *We* change. *We* learn to value ourselves and each other differently. We change our minds about what really matters. We fall in love. Like Fiona and … whatsisname … That's what's … it happens everywhere … and it happens all the time …

All elections do is make visible the changes … that have already happened … to US … to US … the changes that we've already made … to OUR reality … the fuckers on the telly are just counting the beans … Like the banks … they just count the beans … that's all they do … we made money so we could keep making the things … and then … then … all that money … it turned out to be fucking imaginary, didn't it? Champagne's real …

(*He drinks. To Daughter.*) It was my business … your business … it was our future they … and now they expect us to agree that to protect their mickey mouse billions of phoney baloney imaginary cash, we should agree to wreck the real world, the world that we live in, we should agree to believe that it's better for real people to really starve and for real countries to really go broke … than that they suffer an imaginary loss? They actually believe that?

Damn them. They are wrong.

I refuse. I refuse to pretend to believe that the purpose of the world economy is to keep those ten thousand worthless, brainless, criminal bastards ponceing around Davos doing finger-painting with Damien Hirst.

**Bride** Dad … for Christ's sake …

**Dad** Sorry … I'm sorry, Fiona … it's all about the future, isn't it … It's all about who we really are and who we decide we really want to be. So we're here … for Fiona and … Tom … with a wish … a hope …

We have to hope. We can't live … if we don't hope. And if we here tonight can all agree to pretend to believe that … then maybe we really can change the world.

So … I'm here to raise a toast … and I mean it. I do mean it.
The Future …

*Ting.*

## SCENE 17
## SVETLANA PREPARES TO LEAVE

*The Frank MacAvennie Female Staff Quarters*

**Svetlana** Well, Hotel Caledonia. I am finished. I can take no more of your people's failure to live up to their potential. I have seen my last overpriced, undercooked Scottish breakfast. I have dry gagged over my last Lorne sausage. I can't see that this election is likely to change anything. It is finished between you and me. I am going home to work in a hotel in Vilnius and complain about Lithuania instead. Goodbye.

*Gavin returns.*

**Gavin** Svetlana, Svetlana, wait, wait!

**Svetlana** Gavin?

**Gavin** Please don't go.

**Svetlana** Did you come up with a reason for me to stay?

**Gavin** I tried Svetlana. I really did. But I couldn't come up with anything good no.

**Svetlana** Nothing.

**Gavin** Not good reasons. But I did come up with some crap reasons … and I thought – maybe one by one they weren't much but together – maybe they meant something …

**Svetlana** You want me to commit my future to a country for a bunch of crap reasons?

**Gavin** Yes, essentially …

**Svetlana** Gavin, no –

**Gavin** (*desperate*) Okay … I know, I know the weather is mainly pish … okay … but there's half an hour every three or four weeks … of utter utter loveliness … and I like that, Svetlana. And I like our food that takes no fuckin prisoners … and I like the way we drink as if we were gonnae die at any fucking minute … and the way people still visit each other at Hogmanay and the fact that you can see the whole country by train in about five hours and Elgin – have you been to Elgin – it's surprisingly nice and I like the way people have to be pissed to be emotional but once they are emotional they're surprisingly tender and once I heard an old man sing *Flower of Scotland* at the back of an aeroplane as it pulled in to the gate at Glasgow airport and we all cringed a bit but deep down we also all cried a wee bit because he was singing what we all felt when those wheels hit the tarmac and the silly names for football teams – Hamilton Academicals, and Inverurie Locos and Forres Mechanics and The Civil Service Strollers and Oats – we use oats really well and Gardens and Graveyards and Robert Louis Stevenson and WS Graham and Eddie Morgan and The frying of the things … all things friable are fried – if we had a large hadron collider it would be to collect new particles in order to see what they tasted like fried – and I love the way that if you go ten miles everybody sounds different and the colour of stones and Gaelic place names and the fact that not a lot of people are from here so wherever you go in the world if they say 'where are you from' you can have that wee glow of knowing you're not going to give out a boring answer … and all those things are a bit crap Svetlana but I like being a bit crap because it makes me less dangerous … Being Scottish is a mental illness, okay, but so is every other nationality. At least we know we're sick – so ye've got tae give us some credit for the existential feat of creating a positive out of a negative, Svetlana – we are the world champions of desperate last ditch hope which is why I'm going to say one last thing Svetlana one last thing as you clutch your wheelie suitcase handle to leave – the best thing about Scotland right now for me … is that it's got you in it …

**Svetlana** Oh Gavin.

**Gavin** Oh Svetlana.

**Svetlana** You do talk a lot of shite.

**Gavin** What?

**Svetlana** It's shite Gavin … but I do quite like the way you say it …

**Gavin** So you'll stay.

**Svetlana** For a while longer.

**Gavin** Fucking barry!

**Svetlana** Just one condition … we have to get out of this shitty hotel!

**Gavin** What … Now?

**Svetlana** Now.

**Gavin** Are you sure? We don't know what it might be like. I've lived here all my life … it might be dangerous. Do you know what's out there?

**Svetlana** Scotland.

**Gavin** Do you know what it's like?

**Svetlana** No. But it's got to be better than this. Take my hand.

*He does. They exit. Manager enters.*

**Manager** Ho ... Svetlana ... Svetlana! We're getting a terrific response on the leaflet. Folk are crazy for it in New York and Beijing. We're fully booked Svetlana. So you'd better get the Jeanette Krankie Changing Village and Sauna mopped down before the coach parties arrive tomorrow. Svetlana? Svetlana? Svetlana!!!!

*Lights fade to black as The Eagles' Hotel California fades up.*

## THE END

To obtain the rights to perform this play, please contact the Traverse Theatre.

# I COULD FEEL THEM MELTING

## Mark McNay

From the cab of the truck, I could see a stand of cooling towers in the distance. Huge puffs of steam curled into the clouds. As we got closer we drove under monstrous pylons that dangled cables carrying thousands of volts. A mountain of coal was stacked next to the concrete walls of the power-station. Yellow caterpillar trucks crawled over the black as if they were sheep grazing a hillside.

My brur nudged my elbow and nodded at the driver's tobacco. It was wedged between the windscreen and the dashboard.

'Go on,' he said in a whisper.

I looked at the golden lettering on the packet and licked my lips. We hadn't had a smoke since we left London. I coughed into my fist and turned to face the driver. His big hands were wrapped round the steering wheel. His fingers had black hairs sprouting out of them.

'Mister,' I said. 'Can I have one of your fags?'

He looked at me and at his baccy. 'Roll me one,' he said. 'And you can make one to share with your pal.'

I grabbed the packet, and said 'brur.'

'What?' he said.

I nodded to my side. 'He's not my pal,' I said. 'He's my brur.'

When I had the first puff, the taste of it made my mouth water. My brur reached for it straight away, but I held it just out of his grasp. After I had another couple of blasts, he nudged me hard in the side, so I passed him it.

'Are you going back home then?' said the driver.

'Aye,' said my brur as he had a lungful of smoke. 'We're fed up with England.'

'No offence,' I said.

It was more likely that England was fed up with us. We'd only been down a couple of months and we'd been arrested four times. We'd even spent twenty-one days on remand for theft.

'Why did you come here?' said the driver.

'We heard there was plenty of jobs,' said my brur.

My body was rigid as I stared through the salt-flecked windscreen. I tried not to blush. The real reason we'd came was because somebody told us you get better giros when you lived in the bed and breakfasts. And my brur thought it would be easy to nick out the shops.

'Did you find any work?' said the driver.

'Just the odd day here and there,' said my brur.

Truth was, we didn't even try. We spent most of our time smoking draw or scrounging fags off people on the streets. My brur seemed to like it, but I wanted to get home. Maybe see if my da could get me on an apprenticeship or something.

'Times are hard,' said the driver.

'Aye,' said my brur. He sounded as if he was fifty and had spent years working as a labourer. He turned to me and waggled his eyebrows. I tried not to laugh.

The driver didn't notice. He flicked his fag end out of the window and turned to me. 'Who's the eldest?'

'He is,' I said.

'Does he take care of you?'

'Aye.' What else could I say?

'Make sure you stick together,' said the driver He held his clenched fist up from the steering wheel. 'That's how you stay strong.'

My brur leaned forward. 'That's what my da told us,' he said.

The driver tightened his lips and nodded as if he approved. 'We had plenty of your lot come down during the strike,' he said. 'They were champion at keeping us organised. It were like they'd been fed collective bargaining with their mother's milk.'

'Unlike these scab bastards,' he said as we passed a sign that welcomed us to Nottinghamshire. His face was twisted as if he could smell something nasty. He had a long cough before rolling his window down and spitting outside. He wiped his face and leaned into his steering wheel. He drove faster and faster. I heard him mutter about how the country had gone to fuck since Thatcher broke the miners. 'It's every man for himself now.'

We sat in a grim silence for a few minutes. Then the driver pressed his indicator and the truck slowed as we passed a sign that said 'Mansfield'. He bumped onto the verge when he stopped at the roundabout. We said cheers as we clambered out with our stuff.

'Safe trip back to Bonny Scotland.'

I slammed the door and lifted my rucksack onto my back. The coldness of the wind hit me like a punch. We walked from the scrubland surrounding the slip road until we were back beside the dual carriageway. We stood underneath a sign that said:

A1/THE NORTH/SCOTLAND

As soon as we were beside it, I knew it would be hard to get picked up. The motors flew past doing seventy or eighty. They might see us ok, but not in time to pull in somewhere safe. They wouldn't want to risk stopping in case some lorry ran into them and left their car a flattened mess on a telly screen, one dead and one in intensive care.

Two hours we waited, and still weren't getting anywhere. The cars had started to put on their lights, and it made them seem even faster as they flashed by. One peeped his horn and when I looked a guy gave us the fingers.

I turned to my brur. 'What are we going to do if we don't get a lift?'

'Don't worry son,' he said as he faced me. His eyes creased like my da's. 'We'll sort something out.'

I gulped and stared at the joint between the tarmac and the kerbstone. Road dust was washed into it in windswept whirls. It looked like the pictures of erosion the Geography teacher had on the walls at school. As I gazed at the dirt, I imagined I was a cameraman in a helicopter that was sweeping over the coastline of a tropical island, the sands blown into beautiful curves against palm trees and rocks.

'What if a helicopter appears?' I said.

He looked at me and I felt my mammy's cuddles shining from the brown of his eyes. He smiled at the game we'd played since we were wee boys.

'And it has a woman pilot,' he said.

'A rich one.'

'And she takes us to this big house, one of them mansions with trees crowding the gardens and people wandering around eating pieces on cucumber.'

'The sun would be shining,' I said. 'Like the Bahamas or something.'

'And the steaks they'd give us.'

My mouth watered at the thought of biting into one, the juices on my tongue and the aroma of it curling into my nostrils.

I nudged him as a lorry bore down on us. It was close to the edge of the road. We stepped back as it blew past. It roared with the noise of a herd of stallions galloping across the moors. I ducked into the slipstream and felt the spray on my face. I staggered with the force of it, but there was something in it that could hold me up, stop me from falling into the carriageway.

We laughed at each other with the exhilaration of it.

When we settled back down, I noticed the light was fading fast. The traffic was getting less busy, and the cold was eating into my spine. We shivered and stamped our feet, and I thought it couldn't get any worse. Then the wind picked up and it started to snow. My fingers were dead as I gripped my coat round my frame. When cars appeared out of the flurry, we argued over whose shot it was to stick their thumb out.

'Your go,' said my brur.

'No yours.'

'Come on to fuck.'

'No, you come on to fuck.'

The snow didn't last for long. After a while it changed to slush. Big sloppy crystals of it landed on my hair and soaked into my shoulders.

'Imagine a motor with a rich woman in it?' I said.

'Shut up.'

A lorry and two vans flew past. I could hardly see into the distance because the slush was coming down and putting a slippery coating on the road. I half hoped there would be an accident and the police would take us back to the station and give us a cup of tea and a roll on sausage.

It was properly dark before a motor stopped. There was two guys in it.

'Where are you going?' said the passenger.

'Glasgow,' said my brur.

'Jump in,' said the driver. 'We'll start you on your way.'

We piled onto the back seats. It was that warm I could feel the heat toast my cheeks. The passenger lit up a fag then gestured at us with the packet. We grabbed one each and as I puffed on it my head was filled with joy.

The driver nodded his head as The Jesus and Mary Chain rattled out of the tape recorder. They sounded as if they were screaming into their mikes to compete with the roar of the engine and the heater, and the squeaking of the windscreen wipers. The driver pointed at the stereo. 'They're from up your way,' he said.

'I know,' said my brur. 'They're from the same bit as us.'

I frowned because I knew they weren't.

'Where's that?'

'Easterhouse,' said my brur.

I smoked my fag and kept my beaming face down.

'I heard it were rough there,' said the guy. 'Like Doncaster.'

My brur just nodded like he was a philosopher from the slums. He scratched his nose as he was thinking up his next batch of lies. I looked up and saw the driver nudge his mate. I half expected them to start humming the tune to Jackanory.

We were only in the car for ten minutes, when the guy in the driver seat put on the indicators.

'Where are you going?' I said. I turned to my brur, but he gave me his 'behave yourself' look.

'You're not in a hurry are you?' said the passenger.

'No,' said my brur.

I was.

'We live near here,' said the driver.

'We're just nipping back,' said the passenger. 'For a bite to eat.'

'You must be hungry,' said the driver.

My brur smiled at me. 'Starving,' he said.

'I would be,' said the passenger as he nodded to the window. 'Standing out in that.'

'You can come and get a sandwich if you like,' said the driver.

'Sounds good to me,' said my brur.

'We've got bacon,' said the passenger.

'And you can wash it down with a hot cup of tea,' said the driver.

'Brilliant,' said my brur. He nudged me with his elbow.

The car slowed as it hit the slip road. I felt us curve away from the artery that would take us to the heart of Scotland.

I tried to speak but the smoke and the heat made me cough. Then I cleared my throat. 'I want to get out here,' I said.

My brur punched me a sore one on the leg.

'No,' he said. 'We're going with these guys.'

The car drove faster as it turned onto a road that was overhung by trees. I shouted and shook the passenger's seat. 'Stop,' I said.

The men looked at each other and I saw the driver shrugging. He indicated and drew into a lay-by.

'Sure?' he said.

'Aye.'

I pushed open the door and had one foot on the ground when my brur spoke. 'Be sensible,' he said. 'We should get something to eat.'

'We've got chocolate biscuits,' said the driver.

I looked at the driver, before I turned to my brur. He was hugging his bag on the other side of the seat. 'Come on to fuck.' he said.

I stepped out of the motor.

'My da said we should stick together,' he said. His face creased as if he was trying to be serious. 'He'll kill me if I let you go on your own.'

'Well come with me then,' I said.

'I'm the oldest,' he said. 'You should come with me. And it's freezing out there.'

'It is that,' said the driver. 'What you need is some grub inside you.'

'See?' said my brur.

We stared at each other for a couple of heartbeats.

'Are you coming then?' he said.

I shook my head.

'Fair enough,' he said and reached across and yanked the door closed.

The engine revved as they pulled away. I couldn't make out the reggy number because it was spattered in muck. I watched the brake lights brighten as the car went round a corner. When they had disappeared, I stood for a bit, staring into the darkness.

Eventually, a buffet of wind clattered through the roadside trees. I realised I was shivering with the cold. I buttoned up my coat and swung my rucksack onto my shoulders. As I stepped along the verge towards the A1, flakes of slush landed on my face. I could feel them melting.

# NAEB'DY'S CHIEL

## Sam Irving

And when the last trumpit blaws
Wha'll mourn?
When the sodden minds and rag taggery
O this burnt heather clay
Pech tae the Gates
An say tae Peter
It wisnae me
Wha'll be bothert
Eh, Andro?

Wha'll e'en mind
O the proud and ever gubbed
Clan o mongrel herts
Broken banes an lost promises
That used tae pray and rut
And curse their luck
At the hail abominated
Unfair shitey bastirt
Nature o God an his warl
An his bluidy midges
Wha'll care? Wha'll listen?
Naeb'dy, Andro

It's a lang time syne we were enlightened
Syne we wir the sulphur oan the match
It's burnt doon tae the fingers noo
Wha e'en noticed
Wha raised a hand
Mak'd a mell
Pointed a finger

When the acid lies o la'makers
Ate away the country's face
When the needles o commerce
Burst the junkie veins o hope
When the lush and thrusty pelvis
O fitba
Ran oor dreams intae cundies

Wha cares, Andro?
Saint o this parish
You? You're as
Cauld as oor expectation
Frozen as oor vision
Lyin shivery white in the clart
O Loch Lomond
Deid as oor Empire fodder generations
That held the weel-faured spunk
O a great clan
But noo?
Noo
The burns run wi pish
The veins wi stoury shaddies
Oor freedom gliffed
And grued and fleed
Its dreich drizzled hame

Tell me, Andro
You'll ken
Is it aye
The lightest minds float tae the top
Like keech?
Is it aye the wye
Ye fell fowk's bairns in foreign fields
An they loo yir flag mair?
Wiv cam fae a better place
Tae a nippit vennel
A cleared glen
A roundabout in Glenrothes
A civic forum fu o

Weet moos an tume heads
Am ah the only one
That thinks this positively?

Andro, how are ye wi miracles?
Exhume Hume
An set him thinkin
Birl Smith from his Canongate graff
An let him pit the heid in a thae bastirts
For a the ill done in his name
The trumpit echoes roon Craigmillar
Were you ever there, Andro?
And Whitfield?
Castlemilk and Castle Leod are not brothers
Jean Brodie fetch yer tawse
Strap condemnation into thae classroom souls
And force the wee buggers tae think
Tattoo their teeth wi the Declaration o Arbroath
So their smile reminds
Somebody about something

Andro, is that the trumpit
Or a siren?
There's no many o us left clingin
Round yir mingin feet
I've a fiery dram left in me
But the angel took its share
And the rest is fading
We baith need help
Ah ken ye've been greetin
Ye think a chiel
Canna spot a parent's grief?
Gie's yir tears
We'll feed on the salt
An distil the rest tae happy dew
Like a flooer jist growing wild
Christ we're naethin
If no optimistic

# AFTER SCHOOL

## William Letford

Robert Mackenzie had recently taught his son how to walk like a man, shoulders back, head high, spine straight. And Joseph had followed these instructions with the diligence and trust only a five year old could give. But now that he was barefoot, slapping along the side of the swimming pool, elbows flashing outward, every one of his ribs visible, Robert realised the way his son walked looked, well, ridiculous.

When they reached the shallow end Robert went in first and dropped down so his body was submerged. Joseph put his hands on either side of the ladder. There were shouts and splashes but Joseph kept his hands on the ladder and his attention fixed on the water.

'Turn around and come down backwards.'

Joseph turned and put his left foot on the first rung, then his right foot came down to meet it, he put his left on the second rung, and his right foot came down to meet it, he put his left foot on the third rung, and his right foot came down to meet it. He entered the pool in stages and every movement was a task. The water reached the base of his neck and when he turned round he said, 'It's cold.'

'You'll get used to it.'

'I don't like it,' said Joseph.

'Why?'

'I'm feart.'

They'd been swimming before. Two years previous Robert had slipped water wings onto Joseph's arms and carried him into the baby pool. Joseph had screamed, flapping around with a determination that sprung from his desire to escape. The fear was infectious and the other parents were only sympathetic until their own children began to whine. A tactical retreat had been necessary.

'Look at me,' said Robert, and Joseph locked stares with him, walking like a man and the importance of eye contact had been taught as one solid package. 'That's why we're here; beat your fear before you can swim.'

Someone behind Robert dive-bombed into the pool and the guard blew his whistle and Joseph flinched and seemed close to tears. Robert moved closer, he said, 'I'll make you a deal. Every time we come here we can leave as soon as you've done four things for me. Just four things, but you've got to do them well.'

Joseph looked to the right, then he looked around the pool, then he nodded his head.

'Okay,' said Robert, 'we'll get our hair wet.'

Joseph trembled.

'We'll hold our breath and drop down slowly. When the water comes above our noses we'll look at each other and when I blink we'll dip our heads down and get our hair wet. Deal?'

Joseph said, 'Deal.'

Robert let his legs drift out behind him. He took a theatrically large breath and Joseph mirrored him and kept pace with him as he let the water rise above his chin, then his mouth, and they both stopped with the water line above their nostrils. Robert searched for panic. There was no panic. He blinked. Joseph closed his eyes and was gone and back before Robert had ducked down. His hair had flattened onto his scalp and he gulped air and swept his fringe away from his face.

'Just like being in the bath,' said Robert.

Joseph wasn't smiling and he reached out.

Robert slid his hands beneath Joseph's armpits and stood up and lifted him straight out of the water. 'Look at me,' he said, and Joseph looked. 'I'm here. Nothing'll happen. Do you believe me?' Joseph stretched for a cuddle but Robert held him out of reach. 'Do you believe me?' He nodded and Robert pulled him to his chest. Joseph wrapped his arms around Robert's neck and his legs around Robert's waist. 'We're going further into the pool then we'll hold our breath and reach down to touch the bottom, just like that, easy, okay?' Joseph nodded, Robert felt the movement against his neck and walked deeper into the water.

When the depth was right Robert said, 'You know how long you can hold your breath, you've done it in the bath loads of times.'

Joseph was looking down through the water at the bottom of the pool.

'It's too deep for you to stand up,' said Robert.

Joseph kept looking through the water.

'But we'll get down there to touch the bottom.'

Joseph let go. Released the tension in his legs and threw his arms out so he fell straight down. Robert only held him with one arm and he jerked in reaction as he tried to grab him. Joseph's body sent up a splash and his fingers were splayed as he clawed the water in front of him. Robert lifted him out and shouted, 'What are you all about, ya madman.'

Joseph coughed and tried to open his eyes but water streamed down his face. He said, 'It'll no work.'

'It'll no work because you don't know how to do it. I'll tell you how to do it but you can't just jump in.' He slung him over his shoulder and walked into shallower water. 'I'll show you how to get warm.'

Joseph wiped his eyes and blinked at three women sitting with their backs to the edge of the pool. He said, 'How do we get warm?'

Robert took him to the side and put him down and turned so both their backs were against the white tiles. He got down close, 'See these people,' he pointed around the edge of the pool, 'that old man there with the white hair on his chest,' he moved his finger and Joseph's head followed, 'those three ladies all bunched together, and the guy that looks like a frog, with the goggles. All these people know how to get warm.' Joseph looked up, clearly expecting the miraculous, and the expression reminded Robert so much of Joseph's mother that the smell of the chlorine and the water lapping against the tiles and all the voices beneath the high ceiling became garbled. He leant close again, 'Son,' he said, 'there are secret vents around the outside of the pool.'

Joseph scanned the outside of the pool, and stared at the three women. 'Where are they?'

'You have to find one, they're under the water but you'll know when you get to one, you'll feel the warmth against your legs.'

'Do you know where they are?'

'Course I know but you're still going to have to find one. Stick to this end by the wall where you can stand up, and take a walk.'

Joseph didn't seem inclined to move.

'Go for it, I'm here to watch you, hurry up or we'll freeze and be stuck here forever.'

And off he went, in the direction he was facing, shimmying sideways, holding on to the side of the pool with both hands as if there was a sheer drop below him.

He kept going, never moving more than an arm's length at a time, until someone sitting at the edge blocked his progress. Joseph waited. The young guy said something then moved so Joseph could shimmy past and as the guy pushed himself away from the side he looked over toward Robert. Robert gave him a nod and the guy floated backwards, watching Joseph make his careful way along the edge of the pool.

Joseph stopped, and began testing something with his feet. He turned and let go with one hand and waved over. Robert waded through the water toward him.

'It's here,' he said, excited, 'it's pushing me away.'

'Stand in front of it, it'll keep you warm.'

'It'll push me into the water.'

'Don't be daft.' Robert picked him up and plonked him directly in front of the vent.

Joseph reached out with his left hand and paddled desperately with his right, trying to force his body forward, stretching for the edge. Every movement exaggerated, jaw shot forward, teeth clenched, fingers of his left hand wiggling up and down as they searched for that extra centimetre of extension. Clearly he was making a big deal out of it. The force from the vent wasn't that strong. He threw his right hand forward, made a little jump and grabbed the edge. He looked up and said, 'I was almost a goner.'

Robert relaxed and lay back and let the water take the weight of his body. His toes appeared out of the water and he looked at Joseph through the gap between his own feet. He was still holding onto the side, staring down through the water with a look of fixed concentration, pressing one foot against the vent, exploring the pattern with his toes.

'Swimming's the closest thing you'll ever get to flying, Joseph.'

Joseph turned to Robert briefly then looked back down at the grate.

'Not when you're on top of the water, when you're underneath it. You can't be afraid of it. You've got to learn to open your eyes, even in the chlorine, even in the salt.'

Joseph took his foot off the grate and said, 'The water coming out isn't very hot.'

'What did I just say?'

Joseph plunged one hand into the water then let it hang loosely in front of his face, watching water fall from his fingers.

Robert manoeuvred himself into a sitting position. 'Hiy, what did I just say?'

Joseph grabbed hold of the side again.

'Tell me what I just said.'

Joseph wouldn't answer, but he was staring right into his father's eyes.

Robert pointed at his own stomach. 'It's this feeling here that'll stop you. Beat that feeling and you can do anything.'

Joseph blinked a couple of times, but when he blinked he squeezed his eyes shut.

Robert pointed toward the deep end. 'Now walk into the water as far as you can, right till it's above your mouth, right till it's above your nose, then turn back and walk toward me.'

Joseph didn't move.

'Do it.'

Joseph's chest expanded, and contracted, a bit quicker, then a little bit quicker.

Robert shook his head, 'Do it and we can go.'

Joseph released his grip on the side, then walked forward until the water reached the top of his neck. People were treading water, or having a chat, or swimming lengths, or leaving or coming in. Robert took in the whole scene with one sweep of his head. Joseph stopped, but he didn't turn round. Robert willed him forward. Joseph walked a few steps more until he had to raise his chin so his mouth could remain above the water.

Robert stood up and saw he was on his tip toes, arms flailing, finding it hard to keep his balance.

Robert shouted, 'That's enough, turn back,' but before Joseph could struggle round he walked forward and picked him up and said, 'that's ma boy.' He took him to the side and sat him down on the edge of the pool so his feet dangled into the water.

'Do you know how brave that was?' he said.

Joseph didn't look up.

'Look at me.' Joseph still wouldn't look so Robert put his hand beneath his chin and tilted his head back. 'Grown men wouldn't walk that far into water when they couldn't swim.'

Joseph's expression was blank.

Robert stepped to the right, planted both hands on the pool side and hauled himself out of the water. He picked Joseph up and cradled him with one arm so they were facing each other. 'Show me how much I love you?' He said.

Joseph wouldn't react.

Robert raised his voice. 'Show me how much.'

Joseph took a deep breath and pushed out his chest and stretched his arms as far as he could.

'Nowhere near enough.' Robert thrust his him upward so he held him above his head. Joseph closed his eyes and strained to get his hands further apart. Robert brought him back down. 'Now let's do something about that walk.'

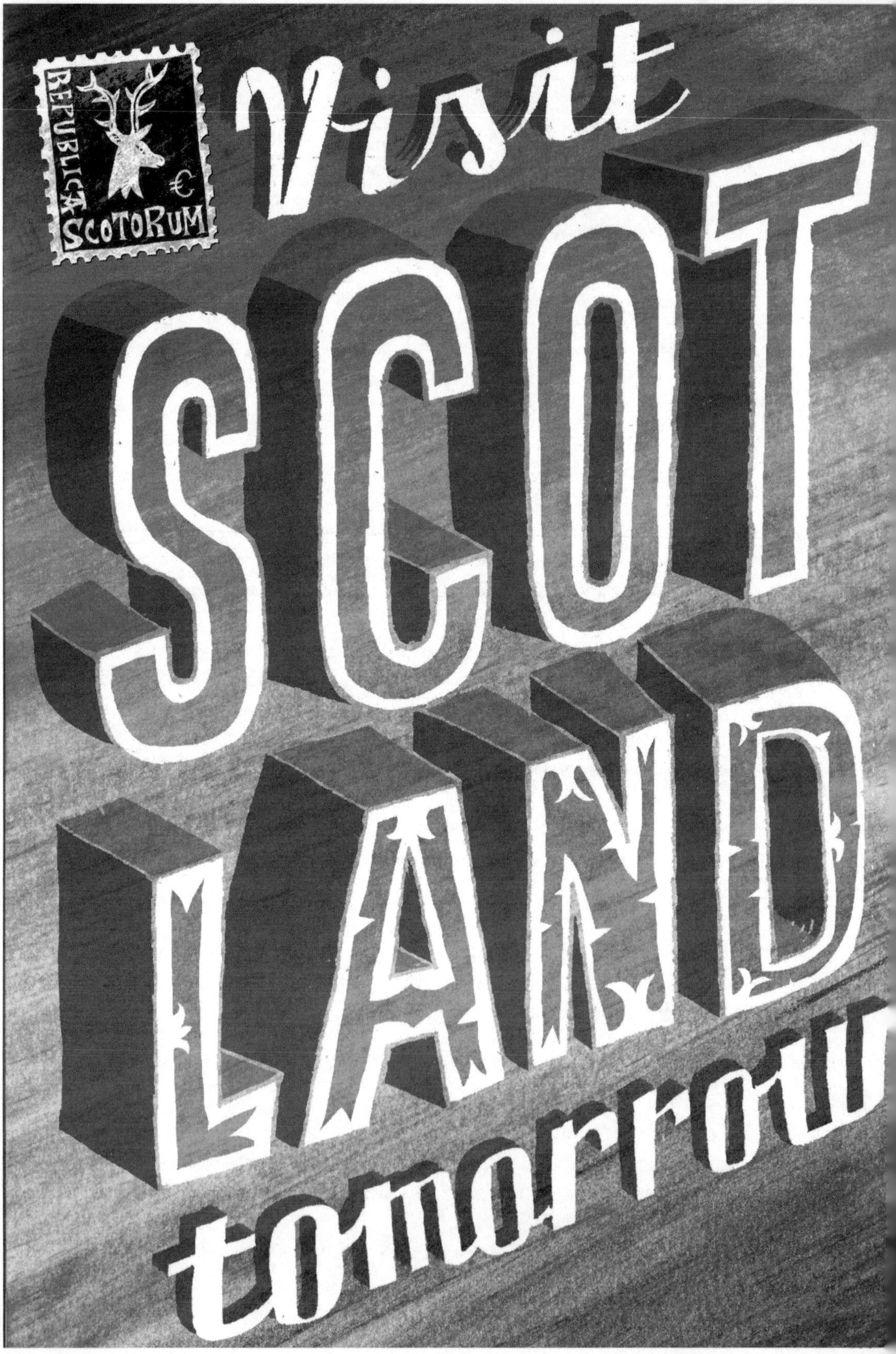
REPUBLICA SCOTORUM
€
Visit
SCOT
LAND
tomorrow

WORLD FAMOUS TOUR DE TROSSACHS

SOUVENIR OF OLD GOMA

SIR CHRIS HOY

# STUAGH-MARA

## Aonghas Pàdraig Caimbeul

Gun Chanute na Gàidhlig
bha sinn bàthte

gun duine a sheasadh
a' bacadh na mara:

cùrsa ar beatha
lìonadh is tràghadh.

Bha Seonaidh againn gun teagamh
a bhiadh sinn a dh'aindeoin –

neo air sgàth – gach bàthadh
's iomadh bàrd a thug dhuinn dàn

na h-aitearachd àird.

                          Ach
chaidh i thairis a dh'aindeoin a' bhalaich

a lorg sinn gus òrdag a stobadh
sa bhalla.  Bha e ro thana – air stàrbhadh

le cinn a bhìdh 's ag ràdh
nach do dh'ith e o linn Chùil Lodair,

's am buntata air lobhadh 's a ' chlann
air siubhal gu cogaidhean cèin. Thuirt

e gun robh dubh-ogha reamhar aige an Aimearagaidh
aig nach robh cead-siubhail, oir bha e

poiltigeach                      mearachdach.

# WAVE OF CHANGE

## Angus Peter Campbell

Having no Canute in Gaelic
we were acutely disadvantaged.

No-one to stand there hand upraised
forbidding the ocean to come further:

our lives were demarcated
by the passage of tides.

Oh, we had the sea-god Seonaidh all right
whom we fed despite – or because –

of the drownings, and so many great
bards to write about the eternal

power of the surging sea.

                         But
it swamped us despite the boy

we found to put his thumb in the
dyke. He was far too thin – claimed

he'd been starved of food and hadn't
eaten since '45, and that the potatoes

had blighted and that his children had gone
away and died in wars overseas. Said

he had a very fat American great-great-grandson
but he had no permission to enter, being

politically                           incorrect.

Choimhead mi air grunn làithean, a' caismeachd
sìos is suas an tràigh, a' togail

bhloighean feamainn 's gan tilgeil
gun mhothachadh dhan chuan. Shuidh

e an uair sin air creig a' feitheamh
ri lìonadh na mara,

a thug cho fada.

                      Aon,
thuirt e, dhà, trì, ceithir, còig, sia.
Agus seachd.

B'e an t-seachdamh stuagh a thaom
thairis air le cop tiugh

geal 's e falbh gun lùths a-mach
leis a' mhuir-làn iar air Orasaigh.

                  Mar sin,
ghabh mi àite, gam chrathadh fhìn

's a' guidhe gach oba sean is nuadh.
Sheinn mi 'Soraidh leis a' Bhreacan Ùr'

's 'Cànan nan Gàidheal' 's ghairm mi
an Rebholution, ach bha gach neach ro sgìth

neo marbh neo trang 's cò an diabhail mise co-dhiù
'son innse do dhuine sam bith mu strì.

Thraogh an cuan,
's thàinig fèath air an tìr.

Sheinn na h-eòin, 's ruith clann le iteileagan
air an tràigh, 's 'as dèidh làimh dh'imlich

sinn uile reòiteagan mìn.

                Nach mìorbhaileach
am muran: an dòigh a cheangaileas

I watched him days on end, pacing up
and down the shore-line, picking up

strands of seaweed and flinging them
listlessly into the sea. He then

sat upon a rock and waited
for the incoming tide,

which seemed to take forever.

                        One,
he said, two, three, four, five, six.
And seven.

And of course it was the seventh wave
which floated over him in white

billows as he struggled helplessly, going
out with the great tide, west of Oransay.

                        So
I took his place, girding my aged loins,

calling up all the new and ancient charms.
I sang 'Soraidh Leis a Bhreacan Ùr', and

'Cànan nan Gàidheal' and called for the
Revolution, but everyone was too tired

or dead or busy and who the fuck was I
anyway to tell anyone which way to move.

The sea receded,
and a dead calm came upon the land.

The birds trilled, and kids with kites ran
along the shore, and afterwards we all licked

ice-creams.

                        I marvel
at the marram-grass: the way in which it binds

e gainmheach ri talamh, gus nach tèid sìon
a dhìth. Tha ar ròpannan a' cumail na mara

fo smachd, 's ma tha ciall sam bith an cànan,
ceanglamaid na sithfeinean còmhla 's mar

a shnìomhas e tron ghainmhich crioslaichidh e
gràn ri freumh gus an seinn  am machaire

laoidh gun tug sinn buaidh a dh'aindeoin na gràin
a bh' againn air gach duine. Thig gach nì

am follais aig a' cheann thall. Dèanamaid ùrnaigh
gum bi sinn làidir anns a' chiaradh: nas treise na crìonadh,
cho treun 's gun cur ar nàbaidheachd iongnadh oirnn,
's gum bàsaich sinn le gràdh a dh'aindeoin stuagh thar stuaigh
's an àite bàthadh sinn a' seòladh nan tonn airson an fheudail

a bhuineadh dhuinn mus tug sinn e gu socair do bhana-dhia
na mara. Na dèanamaid adhradh dhi tuilleadh

fiù's ann am fearg neo mulad.

Thuige seo

's chan ann nas fhaide: tha sinn ga àithneadh, ann an spioraid
Chanute is Hans Brinker, an ainm Dhè.

the sand and holds the land together, so that
no one will ever die. Our ropes hold the ocean

back, and if language has any meaning let
us tie the strands together and, as it winds

between the dunes, do its work of knitting
grain to root until the machair-land sings

that we have done it despite
the hatred we had for each other. It finds

us out, one way or another. Let us pray it
finds us brave: braver than decay, so brave that
we astonish ourselves with our goodness, and die
of love as breaker after white breaker charges, and instead of
drowning  we surf the waves for the treasure

which was always ours before the sea goddess took it
and we bowed down. Let us not worship her anymore.

Even in anger or despair.

                    This far

and no further: we command it, in the spirit
of Canute and Hans Brinker, in the name of God.

# SEACHURCH:
## THREE STATIONS FROM A NORTH-EAST PILGRIMAGE

### Bill Duncan

## (i)
## THE TREE OF UNSAFE INDUSTRIAL PRACTICE: A PEOPLE'S INVENTORY OF INJURY, MAIMING AND DEATH

Sentinel of docklands, monument to the half-light of a dying city's desolation, abandoned by all but the solitary mourner or lone supplicant or derelict in the shadow of dark water's slow lurch against a groan of black timber, faint odour of fungus or faded petals stirring memory.

Seventy-foot mast of a whaleship, marked by time, weather and death; memorial of adventurer, prospector, killer. Improbable shrine, its votive offerings a clamour of signs, each plaque or board a narrative of absence or loss: child colours scrawled in an artless hand, or black script of insect characters burned into a salt-washed board, or perfected anonymity of machine. The bleak newness of day-glo plastic, the peeling and flaking of indecipherable layers, stripped to reveal a cold gleam of scoured metal; a weathered tablet, bleached wood as pale as bone, spectral letters fading in the slow blur of a vanishing narrative. Two centuries held in a palimpsest of narratives made by an unknown author; each sign a tabula rasa, emptied, to be filled with tales told, forgotten, remembered, lost.

Each sign a memorial, nailed to a larger monument: each sign a cryptic remembering, a tale told in a stark, three-word imperative or by a word-less symbol. Archaeology of death, chronology of suffering, archive of pain and loss in a space hallowed by the pagan at the site of a healing tree; a mystery of sacred water worshipped by the Christian; a zone of belief and desire, overlain with mythologies of city and sea. The slow trickle of water, subterranean and on the edge of hearing, named and blessed by St Adjutor, resonant through the lining of stones that root the mast into the well: the thrum of living water still divined through the touch of wood by a delicate hand.

Some nights a tattoo of hail and a drumming of metal, or a seawind shivering its high whistling in the spaces between the topmost signs, or a chord held in a wail of voices, heard for a second that pierces the heart, then lost in the wind.

Tonight a youth scaling the height of the mast, climbing towards the crescent moon in a timeless blue of a maritime sky, garlanding a sign with a circle of white flowers, then vanishing, handhold by sign, foothold by sign, into the slow drift of haar below. Fresh tributes, placed by the hand of a mother, a child, a lover, stirred by the shiver of a seabreeze into a whispering snow of petals, a flurry of memory, sudden, white and lost in the blackness.

# (ii)
# THE FIGUREHEAD OF St ADJUTOR

*Patron Saint of the drowned, those lost at sea, harpooners, navigators, seal-hypnotisers and fishermen*

- the annual spontaneous eruption of barnacles on the face and head of icons and statues in various domestic, church and foreshore locations on St Adjutor's Day – 29th February.

- a slow incursion of haar, at first barely perceptible, but rising steadily from floor to waist height to ceiling, chilling the kitchen of a multi-storey flat with its sudden dampness, muffling the panicked enquiries of the occupants, then vanishing.

- the superimposition of a maritime soundscape, vividly alive with the tidal onrush of surf, wave and the raucous clamour of gulls, upon a wholly alien environment – the waiting room of a funeral parlour, the open-plan floorspace of a call centre, the reception area of the accident and emergency facility of an NHS hospital. Sometimes accompanied by the sharp odour of the foreshore: seaspray and wet kelp. The vanishing of the soundscape as sudden as its arrival.

Unique among the histories of saints is the ardent conviction that St Adjutor moves among his devotees in the maritime communities of North-East Scotland from Dundee to Shetland as a contemporary in the local community. Sightings are not uncommon and are well-documented in the form of photographic and video evidence, most of it gathered through mobile phones in nightclub environments. A prodigious quantity of relics constantly changes hands through a complex network of outlets including dockside bars, harpoon clubs, car-boot sales, gannet-fighting sects, open-air markets and online auction sites. Associated relics include phials of seawater, holy barnacles, porpoise vertebrae, designer-label hooded tops fashioned from an amalgam of technofabrics and intestinal membrane, diviners used to track marine mammals during hunting trips, kayak oars and shaman drums fashioned from seal hide. None of this material, though highly-prized, has been authenticated, despite being the subject of a lucrative and widespread counterfeit industry.

Devotees of the Cult of Adjutor are rumoured to utilise a powerful derivative based on hallucinogenic kelp to enhance visions. Senior members of a tightly-knit sect of kelp users have attained shamanic status and are reputed to sustain reciprocal bonds with a community of Inuits from the area's historic links with the Arctic whaling industry. Beehive structures, fabricated from breezeblock and rubble salvaged from the ongoing programme of the demolition of multi-storey tower blocks, are common in the area and their purpose has been the subject of considerable academic speculation. Commentators have noted a remarkable similarity between the construction of these contemporary cells and the early Christian and Pictish structures which are peculiar to the fields and hills surrounding the housing schemes. More startling is the structural resemblance between these unicameral cells and the igloo of the Inuit and the isolation chambers of Pictish mystics. This effect is enhanced by the use of porpoise and seal hides, sometimes decorated with highly ornate zoomorphic designs, to line the interior. This highly stylised iconography, peculiar to North-East Scotland and to certain Sub-Arctic areas, represents a striking continuity across space and time. Meticulously-rendered charcoal images of sea-serpents, cormorants and seals found in sea-caves near Dundee have been carbon-dated as originating from the Neolithic era. Designs from the same core of images are frequently spray-painted around the desolation of shopping malls and multi-storey car parks in the same area and are used to customise the hooded tops, skateboards and jet-skiers of local youths. Substantial documentation shows remarkably similar imagery embellishing the kayaks and clothing of Inuit hunters. Various incantations have been shared across the cultures and passed down through generations of hunters. Quotations from these verses frequently appear on the distinctive ghost shirts worn for camouflage and decoration. These pre-hunting chants are associated with out-of-body experiences and shamanic ceremonies which are enhanced by kelp ingestion. The rituals invariably precede a hunting trip:

| | |
|---|---|
| *groan of timber* | *creak of spar* |
| *chant of sea-saint* | *sift of haar* |
| | |
| *breath of river* | *rise of moon* |
| *drift of sea-mist* | *wind in dune* |
| | |
| *leap of dolphin* | *plunge of seal* |
| *dive of gannet* | *flick of eel* |
| | |
| *arc of porpoise* | *fulmar's glide* |
| *gleam of salmon* | *selkie's hide* |
| | |
| *net and harpoon* | *lure and reel* |
| *barb and spearhead* | *hook and creel* |
| | |
| *gouge and club* | *and hack and flay* |
| *stab and pounce* | *and gore and slay* |
| | |
| *scale and feather* | *flight and breath* |
| *bone and heartbeat* | *blood and death* |

The meticulously designed acoustic properties of the unicameral beehive structures enhance the repetitive qualities of the incantations which are emphasised by the austere formality of performance: a highly stylised ritual where one voice leads, another follows, then another and another, until fourteen voices converge in a slow blur of sound. The mesmeric effect of the chant is enhanced by echo and repetition, with the performance some-times lasting for an hour or more, frequently inducing a trance-like state in the hunters, whose killing instincts are whetted by the intensity of the communal hallucinatory experience. Bystanders have remarked on the uncanny experience of witnessing the performance: the quiet ululation; the rising ecstasy of song drifting across the fields towards the sea, stilling the riot of gulls to a sudden hush across the quiet of the darkening estuary.

Samples of whale-killing and porpoise hunting often form a core element in the soundscapes created by local youths, who skilfully integrate looped recordings of aquatic mammals in their death-throes with the booming throb of minimalist techno or the crazed syncopation of dubstep. The combination of sound with the holographic aurora of gang slogans, designer labels and hunting iconography projected onto the base of the massive cloud formations that slowly sweep across the desolation of the Northern skies has rendered some observers stunned or speechless for days.

Throughout the early decades of the 21st century, the gentrification of the area's maritime quarters gave rise to a migration of these fishing communities to perimeter housing schemes. Despite this disruption, many of the decanted families, whose tower blocks overlook the sea, still carry on the fishing traditions and enhance time-honoured approaches with technological innovation. Economic hardship, youth unemployment and limited apprenticeship opportunities have led to a core of teenagers from some of these families reverting to hunting on the reedbeds, sandbanks and open water of the estuary. Recent purification initiatives have improved water quality, resulting in a large influx of mackerel shoals into the river, with an accompanying rise in seal numbers. The presence of an increased food supply has also attracted a large resident group of dolphins who have attracted the attentions of the hunters. In the coastal interzones on the edge of the housing schemes seals, porpoises and dolphins form the basis of the sole growth industry in the area for decades. Once the pelts are flensed the skilfully-fashioned garments and highly distinctive bone ornaments are worn by the hunters themselves as well as proving extremely popular beyond the housing scheme. Last summer a disorientated humpback whale strayed into the estuary and promptly became the subject of extensive media and tourist attention. Shortly after the whale mysteriously vanished from the river, a pair of gleaming white jawbones appeared, forming an impressive and monumental archway beside the barbecues, gannet-traps, white plastic garden furniture, seatrout hatcheries, trampolines, harpoons, porpoise-smoking sheds and wendy houses in the back gardens of the housing scheme overlooking the sea.

Local fishermen and marine mammal hunters frequently display a roughly-carved wooden representation of St Adjutor as a figurehead at the prow of their boat. The hunters still attribute their expertise to a steadfast devotion of the saint. In common with fishermen and hunters throughout history and across the world, the instinct to ornament accompanies the urge to work, finding expression in extremely high design values. Many of their artefacts, ranging across canoes, harpoons and clothing, represent an understated but potent unity of form and function. In extreme manifest-ations of the cult, eyewitnesses have observed rituals involving the use of hallucinogenic kelp by chanting teenage hunters wearing beautifully-made ceremonial shirts fabricated from the translucent intestinal membranes of seal, porpoise or dolphin, dependent on the animal being hunted. These ghost shirts provide camouflage in the slowly-drifting haar of the sand-banks. They are invariably decorated with the delicately-rendered religious and zoomorphic iconography of the cult and with words from hunting incantations, fluently drawn with sharpened bone or quill utilising the indelible dye taken from the internal organs of the slain mammals.

While the older members of the communities traditionally favour fishing over sea-hunting, the younger males appear to have moved almost exclusively into seasonal work based on seal, porpoise and dolphin hunt-ing, with their activities tending inevitably toward the clandestine. Some of these youths have apparently inherited considerable divining skills, and employ the traditional cruciform sea diviner associated with the area, fashioned from seabird skulls and willow twigs and fastened with gannet sinew, to track their prey. Historical representations of St Adjutor, from carved seachurch statuary, Pictish stones, stained glass and YouTube clips show the saint in an attitude of stark contemplation, orientating a diviner towards the sea. Youths have skilfully appropriated the cruciform design, with a seabird skull at each point of the cross. Commentators have witnessed the transformation of the diviner from a mere aesthetically pleasing artefact to a supernaturally powerful device that responds to the subtle manipulation of the hunter, leading the subject to hunting or fishing grounds where prey can be tracked and slaughtered. The diviner, though dead and unresponsive in the hands of the uninitiated, functions in skilled hands as a navigational tool as well as an animal tracking instrument and, combined with the camouflage qualities of the ghost shirt, confers a uniquely formidable power upon the youthful hunters of the St Adjutor cult.

A celebrated YouTube archive clip shows a figure in a nightclub dressed in a gleaming translucent ghost shirt embellished with an expertly-rendered sea-serpent, dancing in an ecstatic trance within a mesmerising latticework of stroboscopic white light. The haloed figure moves gracefully across the dancefloor, swaying within a shimmering aura, orientating the sea diviner held delicately in each hand, receiving tributes and salutations from the enraptured clientele. An astonished voice in the background, momentarily audible above the intermittent shriek of the crowd and the pulsating earthquake of bass, can be heard to observe: 'That's him! An that licht's no shinin on him: it's streamin oot o him!' to the gasped agreement of fellow revellers. Indeed, frame by frame analysis shows a strikingly handsome man as conventionally represented in the iconography and statuary of the saint, shaven-headed, fearsome and barnacled.

## (iii)
## THE BAR OF THE FACELESS

Held in profound reverence by its countless beneficiaries, The Bar of the Faceless has provided sustenance for generations of the city's weary travellers. Described by one commentator as 'Scotland's Last Urban Miracle,' the bar is situated across an unpredictable range of ever-varying locations. Its personnel maintain resolute anonymity and the bar itself consists of a disembodied hand emerging from a missing strip of clapboard, a gap in a brick wall or a ragged hole in a rusting sheet of corrugated iron, proffering a modest but welcome alcoholic gift to the passing stranger. Local superstition links the bar with the healing work of the Cult of St Adjutor.

Doubly intriguing is the alternative offering of an apparently random tribute thrust towards the unsuspecting pedestrian, including in recent weeks a litre bottle of Volvic mineral water, a season ticket for Dundee Football Club, a writhing viper and a Wallace's pie. On rare occasions, two hands have emerged simultaneously through fence or hedge, presenting in one instance a fistful of new banknotes and an open razor. One spectacular three-handed offering presented a retired Broughty Ferry primary school headmistress with a triple measure of Navy Rum, The Holy Bible and a loaded revolver.

# POWER OF SCOTLAND

## Helen Jackson

It's ungodly early when Penny skids into line at the rickshaw rank outside Waverley, and near enough pitch black once her dynamo switches off. She rubs her eyes, engages in some half-hearted banter, and buys the first of many strong coffees from the cart. A train from down South pulls in two minutes later.

Penny's fare is a couple on holiday – which is good news. They're too early to check in at their hotel, which is even better. She takes them around to Stevie's left luggage booth on the Bridge and gets them chatting. He's up for the rugby at the weekend, but she's interested in seeing the sights.

'You know,' says Penny, casual like, 'I've a brother works at the Royal Mile 360 Degree Experience. I could get you twenty percent off the entry – and there's no queue at this time of the morning.'

Has she done it? Yes she has! That twenty percent worked its magic, the exchange rate between Sterling and the Pound Scots being what it is. She drops them off, gets the nod from Joanne on door duty, and checks her commission account on her handset to make sure there's a new listing.

Result!

It's straight back to Waverley for Penny – she needs lots of holidaymakers today. She carefully doesn't see the middle-management type trying to flag her down on Cockburn Street. You can't refuse a fare, them's the rules, but no-one's eyesight is perfect.

And, right on cue, there's One-Eyed Rab manoeuvring into the rank in front of her.

'Big date with the new man tonight, I hear,' he greets her, leering. Penny curses inwardly. Is nothing private in this town?

'Jealous are you? When's the last time someone cooked you dinner?'

'Is that what they're calling it these days?'

Two bikes ahead, Kath's listening in. 'You'll need to make quota today, then, Pen.'

'Not a problem. There's a couple from the early train already racking up units for me. Nothing can stop me today.'

The jeers only stop when a new group of fares approaches.

Penny's got her eye on a middle-aged husband and wife in matching anoraks. They'll do nicely, and if she's counted right they're all hers. She just needs One-Eye to pick up the pair of local lads ...

No.

No way!

Rab gives her his toothiest grin as only one man climbs into his rickshaw. The other one's headed for her.

It's stop-start all down Princes Street, more stop than start, which gives her time for the classic visiting-friend gambit.

'Look at the Castle up there. Isn't it beautiful?'

He grunts.

Penny takes it as an affirmative. 'You know, I hardly ever make time to appreciate the city. Are you the same?'

Another grunt.

'A couple of weekends ago I had a pal staying, so I got to play tourist. We did Holyrood and that, but do you know what the best thing was?'

'What was it, then?' He doesn't sound that interested, but at least he's listening.

'The new 360 Degree Experience. It was so cool! I'd not been to a Wheel in years, but that place is amazing.'

'That so?'

'Tell you what. They gave me a discount code – twenty percent off if I visit again this month. I'm not going to have time to use it. Why don't I give it to you?'

'I'd rather make my quota in the gym, or do without the electrics.'

'Honestly, it's brilliant. You're part of a group experience, not sweating away on your own. Give it a go!'

'Nah.'

'I can drop you off there now if you like.'

This time the grunt has a definite negative vibe. Seems like the conversation's over.

Penny stands on the pedals to get back up the hill from Stockbridge. If she can get to the station in five she'll catch the Carlisle train.

Her timing is spot on; she gets back to the rank just as it starts to move.

This time she scores honeymooners. Couldn't be better! They want to go straight to their B&B, but that gives Penny ten minutes to get to work. They're excited and talkative.

'We're history buffs,' he confesses. 'We can't get enough of heritage sites.'

'Ah, Edinburgh's full of the heritage...' Penny's on safe ground here. She can rhapsodise on autopilot while negotiating the lights and avoiding a slow-moving tram pony.

'We wanted to go to the Falkirk Wheel,' he breaks in, 'but we can't afford the entrance fee. We decided we'd stick with one of the Wheels in Edinburgh.'

Candy from a baby, thinks Penny. 'Funny you should say that. I've got a brother works up at the Royal Mile Wheel, he'll give you twenty percent off. Why don't I take you there after you've checked in?' She looks over her shoulder – they clearly like the idea.

'We're part of a reenactment group back home,' he says. 'You know, battles and that.'

Better and better. 'Did you bring costumes for the Wheel?'

They look at each other shyly. 'We've been working on them for months,' he says.

They'll spend all day turning the Wheel! That's a lot of kilowatt-hours. Penny can already picture her commission rocketing. She's certain to make quota at this rate, and that'll give her free electricity all evening. Tonight will be perfect – she'll be the original kitchen goddess. Soufflés to start, she thinks, then a big roast. Maybe Pavlova for dessert. The way to a man's heart, and all that.

Her fare's still talking about the costumes. Based them on *Braveheart*, hand sewn, embroidered something-or-other, blah blah blah. A pause catches Penny's attention.

'Uh ... what's that?'

'Strange how *Braveheart* doesn't mention the Wheels.'

Penny knows how to respond to this. She memorised the official VisitScotland line when she did the Knowledge. 'The movies always get history wrong. Turning the wheel has been an important part of Scottish culture since time immemorial. Back then it'd have been flour mills, of course, but that's not exciting enough for Hollywood. There hasn't been a single film made outside Scotland that features the Wheels. It's disrespectful, is what it is.'

Yep, that's worked. The discussion about anachronism in historical films gets them all the way to the guest house, where Penny is asked to wait so she can take them up to the Mile.

Ker-ching!

Two more couples successfully delivered to the Wheel and Penny's taking a regular customer across town. She checks her commission account at a red light. It's looking promising. As the advert says: 'Powered by the people, for the people'.

'I'm going to have electricity all weekend at this rate,' she boasts. 'It's been all lovers today.'

The fare's an older woman, married with teenage kids. 'What's that all about? I can't work out why people think it's romantic to go to a Wheel. Going round in circles together strikes me as uncomfortably symbolic of the married state.'

'Marriage as a treadmill? I guess you could see it like that. But there's something sweet about working together, don't you think? Making sparks? Creating couple energy? All that stuff.'

The other woman looks disgusted. And, now Penny comes to think about it, she has a point. Hard labour is a passion-killer, however you spin it.

By six, Penny's exhausted. A quick look at her handset and she sees that, although Mr and Mrs William Wallace are still labouring away, she's close, but not quite at quota. It'll be no use going back to Waverley; at this time of day the odds are in favour of tired workers not energetic tourists.

She rounds the corner into Charlotte Square and spots three teenagers with matching language-school backpacks. The one-way system is thwarting their attempts to flag down a rickshaw. One-Eyed Rab's heading round the Square to reach them, pedalling furiously, but she sneaks in before him.

The language school isn't doing a very good job; the three kids pay no attention to Rab's tirade. They squeeze in and ask for *il Castello*.

'*Si si, il Castello?* No problemo!' Penny's Italian is limited. This is going to be a challenge. She gets going, thinking quickly.

'Erm ... *il Castello* is closed? Closed?' She mimes closing a book.

'*Chiude*,' suggests one of the girls.

'Yes ... *si*.' Penny points at the time on her handset. 'It chiude-ed *alla cinque*.'

Okay, this seems to be working. The kids are crestfallen. They flick through their guidebook. Time for Penny to give them some tourist information. Thank goodness she knows the word for wheel: *ruota*.

'Ummm, *Una Ruota? È molta bella.*' Does she mean *bella*? 'Erm, *molta incroyable.'* Damn. That's not even the right language. She pulls up and takes the guidebook, turns to the page about Wheels, and hands it back.

Fast Italian passes between the teenagers. Penny catches the word *ruota* but little else.

'*La Ruota? Si?*'

They nod. Excellent! Penny speeds off before they change their mind. Her mind is refusing to come up with the Italian for discount, so she's going to have to get them into the Wheel without the usual bait.

On the Mile, Penny pulls up directly outside the 360 Degree Experience, breathes a sign of relief, and gets down to shepherd the *ragazzi* through the door. Job done!

The boy wanders off as the two girls struggle with unfamiliar currency for Penny's fare.

'*Si, venti. Venti.* Here, let me.' As Penny grabs a couple of notes, she overhears fluent, if Scots-accented, Italian behind her. It's the Ghost Tour rep and – no way! – he's accosted her mark.

She attempts to herd the boy back. 'Come on, this way. This is the real Scottish experience. Them tours are rubbish. Shite. *Merda.*'

It's no good. Penny's shoo-ing motions are no competition for the Ghost guy's persuasion. She watches her chance of making quota walk away.

What to do?

She's got time to get down to the gym and put in a bit of work on the treadmill herself.

But.

Candlelight's more romantic than electric, isn't it? And he'd prefer carry-out anyway.

OH MAN! THIS IS GETTING TOTALLY RADIO RENTAL!

GET YER PAWS OFFA ME, EEJIT!

WHAT? YOU AREN'T A FURRY? YER A...

THAT'S RIGHT, DOLL!

I'M THE LAST NED IN GLASGOW!

LUCKY WE GOT AWAY FROM THAT PSYCHO STRAMASH! NO MANNERS, THAT LOT! NO LIKE IN MY DAY!

NOO, LASSIE! IF YOU TAKE THIS LANE, IT'LL TAKE YE AWAY FROM HERE! SORTED!

CHEERS, MISTER!

HERE'S SOME FAT LOOT FOR BEING SUCH A LEET KNIGHT! SEEYA, WEE MAN!

OCH! THAT'S PURE QUALITY, MISSY!

CASH TRANSFER: 50 EURO

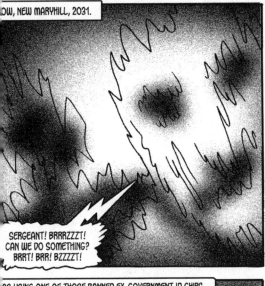

# BUS STOP

## Cynthia Rogerson

*Once upon a time* when the whole world thought innocence was something lost forever and no one claimed to miss it, not really, and no one flinched at atrocities in the newspaper, or was surprised to be out of work, and everyone sighed a lot and if it was a sunny day, said we'll pay for it later – in those weary times, there lived a boy called Angus McNear.

Angus is twenty-two. He still lives on the farm he grew up on, a farm north of Inverness – distant enough so that a trip to town is rare, and he's only been to the leisure centre once, and to the cinema twice. It's his own farm, with no mortgage, and 3,000 sheep all to himself, because his parents' car crashed into a lorry on the A9 when he was seven. At the time, it was a shocking tragedy. When he was older, he realised it was still a shocking tragedy, but a sadly common one. He thinks of the A9 in the same way some people think about certain battlegrounds, and thinks it deserves a memorial, like a war memorial. On his mantelpiece, there's a photo of his parents and himself building a snowman, but he doesn't look at it often. That afternoon is embedded now, and in a sense he still has parents – they just don't grow older. He was brought up by his Aunt Angusina. Yes, yes, highly unlikely. But all fairy tales are based on truth, and those are their real names.

Extraordinary fact number one: Angus McNear has, until last night, never been drunk. Look at any survey you choose, you'll find by age of fourteen, most males in Scotland have been intoxicated more than once. Not Angus.

Extraordinary fact number two: Angus has never kissed a girl. Never been pissed or kissed. Unless you count Zoe last night at the bus stop. Angus, being Angus, does not count Zoe. Why? Is it because she wears skirts that fail to entirely cover her bottom, purple lipstick and her left nostril sports a turquoise star? Is it because when she took the mike last night at Hootenannys and sang *Ae Fond Kiss* off key, she forgot the third verse and sang the second verse twice? Is it because she smelled of cider and cigarettes, and laughed a soft laugh after she landed her purple kiss on his virgin mouth, last night just before he swung himself onto the bus?

No, no, those are the reasons Angus loves Zoe. Angus does not count that kiss because, although it is the pivotal kiss of his life so far, it is not an on-purpose kiss. Angus comes from a hill where they think hard about things before they do them. And so now he is thinking hard about how to find, court, and kiss Zoe properly. And then marry her.

There is nothing else in his mind but this waiting kiss. The air he breathes is fat with his un-given kisses. And his Aunt Angusina's porridge is left cold on the table.

'Are you alright, boy? You've not touched your breakfast.'

'Aye. I'm, fine. Can I have some coffee?'

'You never drink coffee, Angus. Are you alright? Sure you're not coming down with something?'

Angus slowly gives his aunt his brightest smile. She turns from the stove and gives him back the exact same slow-burning smile, with a question in her raised eyebrows. Serious, honest, bright and warm as fire, because she was born on this hill too.

Extraordinary fact number three: Places breed people, just as surely as genes are passed on at conception. Personalities are distilled from places, and this particular high, hard, cold mountain makes people like Angus and Angusina. The high altitude gives them their perspective, not just their view – they see the big picture quicker than the lowlanders. Rarely petty, never mean. Porous, the two of them, and trusting. Wide open to whatever the world shows them. And each night, they sleep like babies.

'I'm not coming down with anything. I'm in love, Auntie.'

'In love? How wonderful! Did you meet her last night?'

'Aye. She's a singer. Her name's Zoe.'

Aunt Angusina laughs a little and blushes, then says: 'Well done lad.'

'I know it's quick.'

'Only takes a second, if it's the right person. Bring her to Sunday dinner.'

'Aye. She'll love your roast dinners.' He looks around the kitchen, out the window at the mountain.

Angusina bustles about, grinding beans and warming the cafetiere. She's wearing Coco Chanel and her outdoor clothes.

Extraordinary fact number four: Even in remote Highland hills, there is decent coffee and often women smell nice when they feed the hens.

Angus glugs his coffee, puts on his boots, gives his aunt's shoulders an affectionate squeeze, and heads down the hill. Hardly notices where he puts his feet, he knows this hill intimately. Walks the twelve miles to the bus stop, rides a bus to another bus stop, then a bus to Inverness, and marches into Hootenannys. Clears his throat.

'Zoe!' he says with gusto.

'Aye?' says Zoe, who is wiping a beer glass. She has dark circles under eyes and a love bite on her neck. She is thirty-two and feeling flat. This isn't what she thought her life would be. Like trudging through porridge, from dawn to dusk. And that waiting sensation – waiting for her proper life to begin. A tease. She'd wither like a bud that the frost killed, before it ever bloomed. A frozen, bruised hard bud. Oh! It isn't fair. Zoe likes to read, and her life reminds her of a book with a shiny cover, a promising first chapter, then ... not much happening. No plot, no suspense, just predictable characters going round in circles. She feels cheated almost every minute. Except when she sings. And she starts to hum right now, thinking of singing.

'You sing great, Zoe,' says Angus.

'How do you know my name?' she asks, reaching for another glass to dry.

'It's me. Angus.'

'Angus. Ok. What can I get you, Angus?' She says his name stressing both syllables. Like a joke. An. Gus.

'No, seriously, it's me. We met last night, remember? I sat right there.' He points to a chair close to the stage.

'You were here last night?'

'Aye. Do you not remember? You kissed me. At the bus stop.'

'Aye, right. So what if I did. What can I get you?'

'Coke please.'

Zoe pours a coke.

'£2 please.'

'Are you singing again tonight?'

'Nah. That was only because I was a bit pissed.'

'You were great.'

'Not. So not. You giving me the £2 or not?'

Angus pulls out a wad of notes. 'I wish I could sing. My auntie, now she can sing. You'd like Angusina. She makes a great pot roast.'

He takes his coke to the same seat and watches Zoe serve customers for the next three hours. By eight o'clock there are so many people, he has to keep craning his neck to see her. She is looking happier now. Some pink in her cheeks.

The music starts and a couple sit at his table. The girl claps and sings along. Dances in her seat. Angus introduces himself, formally, by extending his hand and smiling. At first they laugh at him a bit, but within seconds fall for his earnestness. He is too strange not to like. Just the right side of weird.

He orders some food, Thai food – that's all there is. Ordering is tricky. In the end, he just chooses a number. When 25 arrives, the couple ooh and ah, till he offers them a nibble. Angus cannot decide if it's nice or not. After the third bite, he decides nice. A bit like a Bounty bar mixed up with chilli con carne, without the beans or chocolate. He cleans the plate. His new friends order some too, and when it comes, Angus nibbles off their plates. They are buying each other rounds now, and Angus has swapped coke for beer. He cannot believe how good he feels. Better than Hogmanay and shearing day wrapped up together. The Black Isle Show times a million.

Zoe has stopped noticing him, temporarily forgotten her malaise. Is approaching her beautiful part of the night, where if she is lucky she will attract attention from a man who may – who truly, madly, deeply may – be THE ONE. The way she looks at it, the odds are very good. Look at the world – heaving with single men, and all it takes is one. Her prince is out there, no mistake.

Extraordinary fact number five: Zoe believes in Santa Claus. Or the equivalent of. A cupid who visits the inebriated, making sure true love has a chance. And this regular bout of hope lights her up like a sexy Christmas tree. It also makes her want to sing. It's midnight. The bar has stopped serving and Zoe is on the stage again. She begins with a blues number she learned from listening to Amy Winehouse.

*For you, I was the flame. Love is a losing game.*

She closes her eyes and falls into the sound of her own whispery voice. The pub is crowded and most people are talking, not listening. This doesn't matter. Zoe sings as if her heart is breaking, and Angus sits and listens. When the song ends, he stands up to clap, and whoops and stamps his feet. Some people laugh at him, but when Zoe begins to sing again, people stop talking this time and watch her.

*To knowknowknow him, is to lovelovelove him.*
*Just to see his smile, makes my life worthwhile.*

And when the song ends she stands still, holding the mike, seems lost. In fact, she is a little more pissed than she'd thought, and she suddenly needs the mike for support. Can she sing again? Can she remember what she has just sung? Has any man offered to see her home tonight? What the hell kind of way was this to end a Saturday night? Suddenly, Angus is on the stage, one arm around Zoe, and crooning – there is no other word for it – the words to *Caledonia*.

Extraordinary fact number six: Angus can sing like an angel now, because he is in love.

*I don't know if you can see*
*the changes that have come over me*
*In these last few days I've been afraid that I might drift away ...*

Angus holds the last note and lets it fade away into nothing. The pub holds its collective breath, not blinking an eye. It's eerie. Then Angus swoops into the song again, exactly as if he's diving into the burn on a humid day. The same grace and delicious release.

*So I've been telling old stories, singing songs*
*that make me think about where I come from,*
*That's the reason why I seem so far away today ...*

Another long pause. His eyes are closed now, and Zoe's are open. She looks at his profile, from her position of under his arm, which is looped heavily around her shoulders. The presumption! Did she give permission for him to act like he was her boyfriend? But she can't move, and she can't stop staring at his profile either. And for no reason that's obvious to her, because she's a bit pissed and tired with life, she remembers a long ago day, and walking to school down Montague Row. New shoes, new term, new haircut, new everything. Maybe a hunky new boy has joined her class. Maybe she'll pass maths this year. Anything is possible.

Angus is smiling from coast to coast, and Zoe suddenly knows she needs to throw up. Tries to extract herself from his arm. Angus opens then closes his eyes again, and this miracle voice that did not exist before tonight, hits the perfect notes again. But it wouldn't matter if he didn't because the audience is singing along now. Everyone knows the words to this song.

*Let me tell you that I love you and I think about you all the time ...*

Everyone has just remembered they are Scottish and that Scotland is a lot of sad things these days, and actually a thousand years of sad things, but it is also their own beautiful place.

Extraordinary fact number seven: On Saturday nights in Inverness pubs, it is impossible to be too sentimental. Where this building stands, the ghost of previous gatherings wavers, and also sings out the same song, just different words. People's hearts have been filling and emptying at regular intervals forever. Nothing really changes.

*But if I should become a stranger ...*

'Gonna be sick,' says Zoe, but no one can hear her.

*You know that it would make me more than sad*
*Caledonia's been everything I've ever had.*

And because Zoe's had lots of practice, she vomits in a damage limitation way. Quickly ducks her head to the side, behind Angus. No vomit lands on her shoes or clothes, and she manages to grab a serviette off the nearest table to wipe her mouth.

'You alright, Zoe?' asks Angus under the applause.

'How do you know my name?'

'You told me. Last night. I'm Angus, remember? You kissed me. At the bus stop.'

Zoe squints at Angus. Thinks: Nah, won't do. Too young. Too straight. Not her prince. Pity.

She lets him escort her off the stage, into the room behind the bar. Let's him find her coat.

'Well, thanks a lot Angus. You're sweet. Now piss off, ok?' With a smile – she's not that hard, Zoe. Everyone knows that.

'Now that's no way to talk to your future husband,' he says to her in dead seriousness.

'What the fuck?'

'I said: That's no way to talk to ...'

'I heard you! You mental, or what?'

'You're just tired. And drunk. Let's get you home safe.'

Zoe protests, but the fact is he's right, she is so dreadfully tired right now. And her mouth tastes disgusting, and self loathing is lingering quite close, she can smell it. Like old urine. What word in particular did he say to make her feel limp? She lets him slip her arms into her coat sleeves, and off into the night air they go.


*And they lived happily ever after*

But the ending is never really the ending, right? Not unless someone dies, but even then they can make stuff happen. And the innocence no one claims to miss these days? Of course we miss it, because there's no other way to have it, aside from missing it. Innocence always lives in the past, because we now know what happened next, and then we did not. I can tell you this: One day, Zoe will remember this phase of her life, and see that she was innocent after all. That she truly was, as Angus insisted, a nice girl. And she'll miss that. And the rest of his life, whenever Angus feels a little frightened and alone, he'll sing *Caledonia*. This will calm him, as if he is touching some kind of talisman. It will return himself to himself.

Meanwhile, Angus carefully escorts Zoe past the famous bus stop, over the wobbly foot bridge, and down the wet dark lanes behind the cathedral. He thinks of his hill. His house, the view from his window, his aunt's Chanel, his dog snoring by the stove. The way the air tastes just before snow. The sheep, when it snows hard at night. The way they stand so still, like a group of soft statues. As if conserving all their strength just to keep breathing, buffering each other from the long night. Angus feels twenty years older than he did this morning. How can a single day contain so many changes? To think an impulse kiss can re-direct the flow of a life. Extraordinary. Zoe is quiet now. She is so light and fragile, it is all Angus can do not to simply sweep her up into his arms and plant that kiss right now. But he does not. Tonight is not the night.

# WEE DAVIE BROON AN' HIS FAITHER

## Donald McKenzie

'Whit are ye on aboot Dad?'

'Listen tae whit ah'm saying. Every day, when we went tae school, ma brother wid run away fi me as soon as we were oot o' sight o' ma mither but that niver bothert me cos ah liked tae walk alang the side o' the burn on ma ane – ignoring aw the warnings of course cos ah kent better. On the day ah'm describing ah wanted tae check tae see if ah hud caught any stickle-backs in the bottles ah'd planked in the reeds – but nae luck. Mind you, ah did find a big long chain in the water – an' ah mean big. Pulled it ontae the bank an' hid it in some long grass tae collect later. Funny how ye remember a lot o' stuff ye think ye've forgotten. Ah dinnae ken why but it's one o' those days that hus always stuck in ma mind.'

'Da-ad.'

'Wheeshed. There wus a mad wumman that killed hersel in that burn. Aye – ye're listening noo ah see.'

'Whit did she kill hersel fur?'

'Ah dinnae ken son but the water wis only six inches deep. Ah heard she jist lay doon an' put her heid unner an' held it there. Ah suppose she jist wanted her life tae end cos she saw nae future or jist didnae ken whit she wis daeing.'

'Like Ophelia?'

'Wha's Opheila?'

'Disnae matter. Whit did ye want the chain fur?'

'Ah thoat it wid be a handy thing tae huv but it wis gone when ah went back later.'

'Aye that wis a pity right enough.'

'You wanting a skelp?'

'Naw.'

'Whit's a stickleback when it's at hame?'

'Ye're ignorant so ye are. It's a wee fish wi three spines sticking oot its back.'

'Aw – right.'

'Ye're trying tae divert me. Dinnae think ah'm no up tae yer tricks. Anyway, tae get back tae ma point – an' being ignorant plays a part in it. Ah ...'

'Kin ah put the tele on?'

'Indeed ye cannot! Stop interrupting. Ah'm attempting tae explain something tae ye. Ye'll thank me later.'

'Whit age wur ye?'

'Aboot ten.'

'Kin ye no get tae the point?'

'Okay. Forget whit ah said. Noo, whit ah wis gaun tae say wis that the day before the teacher telt us tae learn a bit of poetry fur oor hamework.'

'An you hudnae?'

'Aye, ah hud. Listen – ah'll no tell ye again. Whit we didnae expect wis that she wid start gaun roond the class asking each of us tae stand up an' recite what we hud learnt – though that wis obvious if we hud thought aboot it. See when ma turn came – ma mooth went dry an' ma mind was racing.'

'Jist the opposite o' that wumman that droont herself then?'

'Right Davie – ye're definitely on a last warning! Ah don't know how but suddenly whit ah hud learnt aw came back tae me. An' ah kin still remember the poem tae this day.'

'Goan then.'

'*The wind wis a torrent o' darkness among the gusty trees,*
   *The moon wis a ghostly galleon tossed upon cloudy seas,*
   *The road wis a ribbon o' moonlight o'er the purple moor,*
   *An' the highwayman came riding*
      *Riding-riding–*
   *The highwayman came riding, up tae the old inn-door.*'

'Obviously ah didnae ken aw the poem but whit ah hud learnt wis okay. However, Billy MacTaggart wis looking decidedly fidgety.'

'Wis he one o' yer mates like?'

'Aye, he wis the class dunce; man he wis thick. We aw kent the poetry wid be a problem fur him but we liked Billy as he wis quite a funny guy. He lived nextdoor an' often ah could hear his mither screaming at him tae get his hamework done – usually followed b'loud bumps an' skelps when his heid wis ricocheting aff the wa'. Well, his turn wis fast approaching an' eventually an' inevitably the finger wis pointed.

*Stand up Billy*, said Miss Gourlay – she wis oor teacher. He stood up in silence, an' it wis a silence that wis frightening.

*What's your poem?* she asked.

Ye could sense the brooding evil hush she wis creating.

*Well?*

*Ah dinnae ken any poems miss*, says Billy.

*You must know at least one poem boy!* she said, aw hoity-toity an' menacing like.'

'Whit did he dae then dad?'

'Well, there wis anither period o' really embarrassing quietness but suddenly a look o' great joy came across his face – an' smiling like a wee angel he blurted oot, *Rub a dub dub three men in a tub*. The place erupted wi' howls o' laughter an ah thoat ah might pee masel. But the teacher wisnae happy. Her face wis wild as a maniac's. Ah thought she wis gaun tae go totally berserk an' she telt him tae come oot tae the front while she went awa tae the classroom next door tae fetch a tawse.'

'Whit's a tawse?'

'A leather strap, a belt tae punish him wi.'

'Ah didnae realise ye were that auld dad. Ah thought they did awa wi that long ago.'

'Aye well, it's no that long ago. There wis some right twisted individuals that we wur taught by ah kin tell ye!'

'So, whit happened next?'

'Well, while she wis away we tricked him; suggested that if he licked his haunds he widnae feel the pain. Ye'd think he wis licking a plate o' jelly the way he slavered o'er them! The anticipation in the room wis electric. Then hersel came back an' telt him tae raise his hands th'gither an' as she swung the belt he jumped back twa feet an' the belt missed. This happened twice an' by then she wis raging, her face even mair red, an' looking like a balloon fit tae burst – but then he ran oot o' space. He tried tae jump back anither time but the wa' wis jist at his back an' ah kin still remember the noise the belt made as it smacked his haunds. It wis like the crack o' a whip. Never mind him hitting the wa' – he jumped that high we thought his heid wis gaun tae hit the ceiling!'

'Aye, very good dad but whit's yer point?'

'Whit's ma point? Ah'll tell ye something son. There's nae industry left; nae shipbuilding, nae mining an' nae steel making. Ah ken my future's aw behind me but if ye're wanting tae get oan an' huv some expectations ye better stick in at school an' get a guid education an' some culture like ah did.

Education. That's whit it's aw aboot – ye need brains tae get on nooadays. Whit this country needs is getting back tae the times when oor education system wis the envy o' the world.'

'You oan yer soapbox again?'

'Listen. If we hud oor country back an' there wis a bit o' pride an' interest in who an' whit we are we wid be very well off. We're jist as capable as the likes o' Norway or Denmark or any ither country the same size. Crivens – Iceland has hardly any folk compared wi' us an' they seem tae manage. Scotland wis at the forefront of the Enlightenment an' it's mibbae time we hud anither. Ye should be looking tae things like science an' the arts, question an' challenge the way things are. That's the way ahead, dinnae rely on these daft reality shows or think ye're gaun tae be some sort o' celebrity because the chances are it's naw gaun tae happen. Believe me – ah've heard ye singing!'

'Ah've heard you singing annaw.'

'Aye – well – ah rest ma case.'

'An' whit if ah dinnae want tae go tae university?'

'Ah'm no saying ye should but it disnae matter whit ye hope tae dae; plumber, brickie, cook, even a job in the Cooncil, ye still huv tae huv some wherewithal tae make a success o' it. You go anywhere in the world an' ye'll find a Scotsman up there wi the high heid yins. It's guys your age that'll make a difference an' whit kind o' future you huv is doon tae you.'

'But you wur lucky dad. You wur able tae buy a hoose an' huv a job guaranteed fur maist o' yer life – an' a pension. It's no like that noo.'

'Ah suppose ye huv a point but that disnae mean ye jist accept it. Ye huv tae get oot there an' change things fur yersel.'

'Like these students that wur rioting?'

'Well – strangely enough ah hud a bit o' respect fur them – no the nutcases of course – but mibbae it wis a sign for the future. Mibbae the worm hus started tae turn. People kin only staund so much. When they see whit's happening – aw these scoundrels in high places an' in the banks laughing at us, oor fishing fleet being decimated, oor oil stolen, the landscape gettin' scarred wi giant pylons an' wind farms being built by 'tak the money an' run' merchants, it's inevitable that thur will be a backlash. Who wud huv believed that politicians wid be trying tae keep us aw in a constant state o' fear an' try tae control us wi the threat o' terrorism here in Scotland o' aw places – a situation they created ah might add but are daein nothing aboot. Cake an' theatre might have been haudin' things in check up tae noo but the price o' breid these days an' the rubbish that's on the tele isnae daein it any mair.'

'Talkin' o' which – kin ah put the tele on noo?'

'Whit's on?'

'The Olympics are startin'.'

'Huv ye been listening tae me?'

'Aye dad – ah hear whit ye're sayin – an' ah agree.'

'Well – jist so ye know it's doon tae you in the end but ye'll get aw the support that me an' yer mither kin give ye. Aw we ask is that ye stick in at the school.'

'Thanks dad.'

'Olympics did ye say?'

'Aye.'

'Whit did ye no say earlier fur? Get it oan then.'

# ONE HUNDRED YEARS OF WIFEHOOD

## Kirsty Logan

## 1951

The blankets feel heavier than icebergs across Margot's hips and even the baby's cries cannot lift them. Margot knows how sound travels through the chipboard walls: the neighbours will be tutting, and if she's not careful they'll tap at the door again, crooning *may we borrow a wee cup of flour?* and *has the postman been by?*, craning over her shoulder to see what's past the door jamb. This fear is enough to lift the blankets.

Margot shivers into her housecoat and goes to coddle the baby. The house smells of burnt coffee and warm milk, and she checks the grandfather clock to see how much time she has to clean up before Alastair gets home. A quarter past eight, says the clock. She realises she forgot to wind it.

Margot cradles the baby and wonders how she can still stand upright when she's already given half of herself to this wriggling mass of puffed skin and soft gums. The house is too cold and the baby's room is too hot. Margot hears the too-slow tick of the grandfather clock, the whisper of next door's wireless, the arguments of birds. Everything is drenched in pattern and she can't focus on any of it so she stares down at the baby's face until her heart slows, until the baby quietens and blinks back up at her. Why did she pick out green and blue flowers for the wallpaper in here? How can the baby sleep with such noisy walls? Who is this creature in her arms and what can it possibly solve?

The baby has sunken back into sleep. Margot tucks it into the cot, folding in the edges of the blanket like the crusts of a pie. She strokes the baby's soft, sparse hair back from its forehead and waits for it to settle. She goes back into the bedroom and lies down on the bed.

Margot passes Alastair the butter for his potatoes. They only have a few ounces left and they are not due more until next rations, so she will have to have her toast dry tomorrow morning. She does not complain about this, and she thinks that maybe that is what love is. Not the hitching of breath and the thumping of hearts, but the concern of another before yourself.

Margot thought she knew what love was before she met Alastair. With Dorothy, the world glittered. Drinking tea on the back step, ragging one another's hair, rolling down hills, even eating dinner with Margot's family: everything was lightness and joy bubbling up out of her throat. Female friends could understand one another the way a man never could. That's what they were – friends. They'd practised holding hands and kissing and more, things that Margot tried not to think about because then she forgot to breathe.

'Pass the salt, please,' says Alastair, and Margot passes it without looking. 'How was Georgie today?'

'Yes,' says Margot.

Alastair clatters his cutlery down on his plate.

'Margot, are you even listening?'

'Yes.' With an effort, Margot lifts her eyelids and looks at Alastair. 'I'm listening. Georgie was fine. I was fine. Everything is fine.'

Alastair reaches across the table and curls his hand around Margot's fingers. 'Dear, what's wrong? You haven't been yourself lately at all. Are you overtired?'

'Yes, I...' But it's too hard, she can't keep her mind focused on the shape of Alastair's chin, and his mouth is moving but she can't follow the words because she's thinking that Alastair is a good man, an honest man, his blue eyes steady and his feet flat on the floor. He never makes her breath catch like Dorothy did but that is as it is – girlfriends are fun, but marriage is a full-time job. It's not as if she could have made Dorothy her husband, and two friends making a life was just too hard. It was easier this way. It was better. She just got tired, that's all.

## 2051

The museum is set up like a house from the 2000s, all manual kitchen-ware and flashing electronics and huge clunky TVs. It even smells authen-tic: over-vacuumed carpets and roasting meat. Priyana thinks she catches the scent of 'air freshener', though how squirting chemicals into the air could freshen it, she doesn't know. It smells like a mixture of lilies and washing powder.

The museum has barriers to keep patrons from touching things, but that never stops a child from doing anything. Priyana has to hold both Avery's hands in her own to make sure all the youthful extremities stay still; she hopes that Mur is taking the same precautions with Taya.

'You can't touch people's things, Avery.'

'They're not people's things. They're the museum's things and the museum is not a person.'

'They belonged to someone once, and you know to respect that. Don't bother with things you don't need.'

Avery shrugs an acceptance and bends over the info screen for the kitchen exhibit. Priyana relaxes her hold on Avery's fingers and looks around the room, trying to imagine what it would be like to live back then, to have desires and curiosities and revulsions back then. Fifty years was not a very long time, and she knew that her dads would remember it. Papa B had waxed lyrical about his youth on many occasions, but Papa M did not speak of it. Priyana knew that Papa M's mother had been unhappy then, and she suspected that his silence was a hangover from that time. No one talked about unhappiness then and so Papa M did not talk about it now. Things must have been very quiet in Papa M's childhood.

Priyana strokes her thumb across Avery's hand absently. She just can't do it: she can't imagine herself in a 2000s wife's place. Fifty years is not long in terms of numbers, but the whole world can shift in that time.

Priyana feels a hand on the small of her back, and turns to face Mur.

'Did you see the iron?' asks Mur.

'Is that like a mangle?'

'Of a sort. They used it to flatten clothes.'

Priyana slid her hand around Mur's shoulders. 'Mur, my love, nothing could make me happier than looking at a clothes-flattener with you.'

'Why are they all the same?' says Avery from behind them. They turn to see Avery and Taya staring into the display.

'Why are what all the same?' replies Mur.

'Those dolls.' Avery nods at the models.

'I think they're meant to be people, Avery. They're dressed up like people in the past, see? Doing their tasks and moving about the house.'

'Yes, I *know*.' Avery twitches a toe towards the edge of the barrier. 'I mean, why do all the people look the same? There are only two sorts.'

'That's not true!' says Taya, pointing at the models in turn. 'There are lots. Five six seven eight people.'

Priyana notices that the models are all very clearly male or female. It's nothing as simple as half wearing skirts and the other half having short hair, but there's something intangible about each figure that clearly places it as either a man or a woman. The spaces they occupy, the angles of their legs and arms, the expressions on their faces: each is female or male.

'You're both right, my loves,' Priyana says. 'There are lots of people and they do all look similar. But that's how things were then: everyone was either this or that, one or the other, with nothing in the middle. You see?'

'Yes,' says Avery with a frown.

'Am I?' says Taya. 'Am I one thing?'

'You are many things,' says Mur. 'Everyone is lots of things. They always have been. But it hasn't always been so that people can be open about it.'

Avery and Taya frown at the display.

'Think of it this way,' says Priyana. 'You play dress-up, right? And you can be a doctor or a firefighter or a mechanic. You can make cakes or knock down buildings. You're all of those things, but you're still you.' She waits for Avery and Taya to nod. 'In those times, the time of the museum, people couldn't do that as easily. There were only really males or females, and they had to do things that fit into those groups. Sometimes females could do male things, but they couldn't do them with the same freedoms, and they could even get called names. Males could do some female things, but they didn't have much freedom there either, and people made fun of them.'

They all stare thoughtfully at the models.

'That's silly,' says Avery, and turns to go into the next room.

# 1951

Georgie grabs for the bee as it buzzes past, but his pink fists aren't fast enough. Margot tips back her head and laughs at the look of rage creasing across his wee face, then shakes a rattle in front of him as a distraction.

'You don't want that nasty buzzy thing, no you don't,' she sings, shifting around so that the sun falls across her shoulder without shining in Georgie's eyes. It's hot on the back of her dress, warming her right through to the bones. Above them the sky is as flat and blue as a china plate. Margot holds Georgie under the oxters so that his bootied feet rest on her knees, then twists him back and forth in a dance. She leans into him after every twirl to blow against his belly. His cackles are loud enough to startle birds from the tree beside them, and Margot holds him up to see the pattern of their retreat.

Alastair is up to his elbows in rose bushes, his hands wrapped in fuzzy green gloves, his shirt open to show his vest. He sweeps his forearm across his sweating hairline, leaving an earthy trail on his face. Margot's smile tips wider: she hitches Georgie up on her hip and sways across the lawn towards Alastair.

'You've a smut.' She leans down, wipes it away with her thumb. Georgie puts out his arms for his father and Alastair plants a kiss on the top of his tufty head.

This is happiness, Margot thinks. She tries to imprint every sensation on her brain: the sun on her back, the smell of the roses, the warm weight of Georgie in her arms, the glowing ember of contentment in her chest. She tries to contain it in a little sphere deep inside her, so that the next time she gets overtired she can hold this moment and let it heal her. Margot tips her head to the sky and smiles so wide that her cheeks feel like table-tennis balls.

'Is he all right to be out in this sun?' Alastair has already turned back to the rose bushes, and Margot's cheek smarts from where it has been denied its kiss.

'I'll go and put his sun hat on.'

She hoists Georgie up on her hip and walks up the back steps. The white paint is starting to chip off the railing; she thinks about calling over her shoulder to ask Alastair to fix it, but she does not.

She can be happy. She just needs to try harder. Alastair is trying, isn't he? He's even agreed to take the baby for one night a week so that Margot can visit Dorothy. The thought of seeing Dorothy makes her feel lighter, fuller, like a pudding rising up over the edge of the baking tray. Soon Dorothy will have a husband too and they can talk about it, about how love is never what you think it will be but that doesn't make it any less like love. About how life is not the way it's shown in the pictures but you never see true happiness in the pictures anyway, just a feeling that flits past. Love in the pictures can't be real because there always needs to be someone to repaint the railing.

## 2051

Priyana stretches her legs out along the couch, feeling the muscles in her calves tense and release. The house smells of old wood and something warm and sweet from Avery's wash. Mur is in the kitchen saying good night to the neighbours on the i-eye and the children are reading in bed; Priyana has set their lights to go off in fifteen minutes. She spoke to this month's neighbour family on the i-eye this morning over breakfast, so she won't join Mur to say goodnight. She knows that they're Russian-born but now live in Sri Lanka, that Tati's cousin is coming over for dinner, that Aleks has a cold, and that their oldest – Priyana never caught the child's name – is having a friend round to sleep over.

In the main room the i-eye is off and the constellations are on; no matter how many times she sees them, Priyana never tires of the tiny lights strewn across the ceiling. Mur pads through to the couch and stretches out next to Priyana.

'I'm glad we took this week off together. Do you want to claim it back? The mental health allowance is up to ten days now.'

Mur shrugs. 'We could. But we have enough for the necessities already. Why have more money than you need?'

Priyana tucks her hand into Mur's and tumbles them both down onto the floor, curling her body close and pressing her nose into the curve of Mur's neck. With Mur, every night is starlit.

'Hello,' says Mur with a laugh.

'Do you think they were different?'

Mur dapples kisses along Priyana's cheek. 'The museum people? No, I don't think so. People weren't different but they saw things differently. They used homes like cages to trap women, not like steady blocks that you stand on to reach higher things. People didn't know how to be different things at once.'

'Do you think they were happy?'

'Sometimes they were happy, sometimes they were unhappy. Just like now. But I think we can talk about it more.'

Priyana thinks about her Papa M, so caught up in the past that he can't even discuss it. She thinks about how it must have felt to be caught in a home instead of making one for yourself. She thinks of a world where people viewed one another with suspicion, where they worked for groups of strangers instead of for themselves and their families, where they collected more piles of printed money than they could ever need: a world before everyone had their own business and enough food and space. She thinks of how this country, her country, considered locking its doors; blocking itself off from new thoughts and words and ways of being. Priyana knows that world existed, but she just can't see herself in it.

Mur stands, pulling Priyana to her feet. 'Bed?'

Under the electric stars Priyana kisses Mur, slow and long like when they first met.

'You go ahead. I'm just going to get some air.'

Priyana sits on the back step, looking up at the sky – the real one, not the constellation on the ceiling. She can't tell which lights are stars and which are satellites. Things aren't perfect, she thinks, because nothing is ever perfect. But it's better than it was, and it will be better again for her children, and for their children, and maybe in 50 or 1,000 or 10,000 years it would all be okay.

Turning to go back inside, she notices that the white paint is starting to chip off the railing. That's okay, she has the rest of the week off. She will repaint the railing tomorrow. No, she thinks: she and Mur will paint the railing together.

Hermless, hermless.

There's never nae bother fae me

I ging to the libry, I tak oot a book

And then I go hame for ma tea.

Michael Marra (1952– ), *Hermless*

# THE SHAPE OF THINGS TO COME
## SCOTLAND'S PLACE IN THE FUTURE

### Gerry Hassan

*Just imagine what it was like when the airship was invented. What a wonderful thing, people thought, to be able to travel through the air just like a bird. And then it was discovered that the airship was a dead-end invention. The invention that survived was the aeroplane. The moral of the story is that in both philosophy and the sciences you must be very careful not to fall in love with your own airship.*

Umberto Eco, in *Predictions: Thirty Great Minds on the Future* (2000)

Welcome to the Future. This is the world of Scotland and its future explored through the power and reach of stories. Taking us into a different place: the imagined world of Scotland's future.

There is today a positive story of humanity, its continued advance and progress. Since 1980 the world is three times richer, while trade in industrial production has risen by a factor of twenty-five. There are more nation states than ever before, fifty in 1945, just under 200 today, and more political democracies than ever before. The last three decades have seen an explosion in technological innovation: the explosion in the internet, computers and mobile phones which has changed business, government and human relationships making us more inter-connected than ever before.

This age of unprecedented change has also been not surprisingly marked by a sense of anxiety, doubt and concern in many circles. The scale of change has also been disorientating, with many feeling they have gained and many lost. Large parts of the West, whether in Europe or North America worry that it is in irreversible economic decline and unable to meet the rising challenge of China, India and emerging economies.

Perhaps even more profoundly there are widespread questions about the viability of long-term economic growth and the issue of the limits of growth, environmental degradation and sustainability, and concerns over global inequality and injustice which are at record levels within nations. What this amounts to across parts of the West is a crisis in belief in progress and in a better tomorrow: in short the idea of the future.

Scotland is no exception to these times, yet at the same time society, public debate and our wider culture and politics find themselves both influenced and shaped by this mood, while increasingly also marching to a very different beat to the rest of the UK.

## The Context: A Scottish Wave of Change

The balance between the bigger picture of the economic, social and financial environment, and where Scotland sees itself heading to and how it sees its future is a fascinating and real one. It is in this context that this book has been planned and conceived, as part of an ambitious project entitled A Scottish Wave of Change which is part of the Cultural Olympiad.

This initiative has begun a series of conversations, dialogues and exchanges exploring the values of people in Scotland and the values they wish to support and nurture in the future. It has done so drawing from as a starting point the seven Olympic and Paralympic values of courage, determination, equality, excellence, friendship, inspiration and respect. People have used these seven values to address what kind of Scotland, community and places they would like to inhabit in the near-future, and how they see themselves being active agents in bringing this about.

What this has entailed is a range of events, discussions and activities up and down Scotland which have invited people to begin imagining and then taking steps to create their own future. This has been called mass imagination and the act of democratising the future.

A Scottish Wave of Change has supported and aided the creation of three local futures projects, in Govan, Glasgow, Dundee and Lochgilphead. Each of these, starting from the same point of the Olympic and Paralympic values has begun a set of conversations about the values they wish their communities to be shaped by in the Scotland of the future. Each has then chosen to develop this in different ways, using film, theatre, music, learning journeys, summer days on the green, and other ways of expressing oneself and making connections. And using the idea of story to animate and make real all of this.

We chose three local areas for a number of reasons. One was to have a long-term relationship with a number of communities, and allow the conversations, processes and outputs to have a chance of developing impact, influence and wide audiences. Another was that in a small way we wanted to reflect the idea of 'three Scotlands': the diversity and differences of our society geographically, generationally and in socio-economic terms. And we wanted from these local futures and visions to be able to draw together a number of strands: to develop specific local initiatives, draw these together into a national picture, and do so in a way which has an international impact.

A Scottish Wave of Change's activities aren't just restricted to Govan, Dundee and Lochgilphead. There are a host of other activities as well: stories, music, theatre, film, young people sailing around Scotland in a boat, the East End Endeavour, collecting and creating stories. All of this is about stories, imagination, conversation, connection about change and the future. This book is but one part of this, including a national story competition and commissioning of specific pieces, with another book to follow next year.

## A Short Guide to the Future

All of this is of course happening at a time of enormous change and flux in Scotland and further afield. These are fascinating and fast moving times for Scotland. After a decade plus of devolution we now have a majority SNP Government which has changed the political landscape of the country. This has brought to the fore the issue of Scotland's constitutional status and the issue of independence.

Even more profound is the wider Scottish desire to have an open-ended conversation about our future, our collective and shared future. And to answer or at least acknowledge the question about what kind of Scottish society would we like to live in? What kind of priorities, values and choices do we aspire to, how do they reflect the wider constraints and environment, and do we have the capacity and energy to enact them?

Scotland's story these last few decades has been a distinct and revealing one. Scotland has more and more chosen to emphasise its distinctiveness and difference as a nation, community and space, both from England and the rest of UK. This can be called the narrative of difference, in that we actually know in-depth that Scotland isn't that different from England and the rest of the UK in terms of social attitudes and values, yet at the same time, as a nation and in how it expresses itself, it feels very different.

This is a paradox which needs to be explored. What is it about Scotland that is unique, different and that people want to cherish and celebrate? What might be unique about Scots that we don't want to retain, but want to challenge and change? Is it still possible to talk about distinct Scots traditions, whether it is 'the democratic intellect' or the language of 'we are a' Jock Tamson's Bairns', all of them informed by a populist egalitarianism in a society which in other respects is shaped by authority and institutionalism? And can we still talk about national values in an age of globalisation and interdependence?

Part of the answer can be found in the richness and diversity of Scotland's voice in the world of cultural imagination, in arts and literature, in writers, artists, playwrights and imagineers. Robert Crawford in his *Scotland's Books* (2007) wrote that, 'The challenge for Scottish literature today is to engage not just with Scotland, but with the world' and that is what writers have been increasingly doing for the last three decades from the annus horribilis of 1979. Such voices have given vivid expression to a society far removed from the monocultural, monochromatic land of the past and embraced Linda Colley's observation in *Britons: Forging the Nation* (1992) that 'Identities are not like hats. Human beings can and do put on several at a time'.

This Scottish journey comes at a time when how we think about the future, and indeed what kind of future, is itself undergoing dramatic change. Thinking and imagining the future is central to the human condition and what it is to be human. From the beginning of homo sapiens the ability to transfer knowledge from one generation to the next emerged, and with it a host of human abilities and creations: the development of consciousness, understanding the consequences of actions such as starting a fire, conceiving of an afterlife, god, religion and language. And as Jacques Attali points out in *A Brief History of the Future* (2009) humans for the first time began to imagine the possibilities of the future.

As humans evolved so did how they thought of the future. There was the long tradition of dreaming of and conceiving idealised communities and the notion of utopia seen in the works of Thomas More and William Morris. More's *Utopia* (which gives the word its modern meaning of 'no place' and 'a good place') and Morris's *News from Nowhere* are both like blasts of dreaming from another age, creating a pastoral, idealised world of perfect harmony and relationships.

Then in the 20th century came the modernist version of the future. This was big, powerful, all-encompassing and suffocating. There was the Communist version of the Soviet Union, the Fascist vision of Nazi Germany and Italy, the ideas and systems of the Cold War and both blocs, and the free market revolutionary thoughts of von Hayek and Friedman. What all of these had in common was a belief that the human spirit was eminently pliable, porous and malleable, and could be radically redesigned by economic and social engineering.

The modernist vision of the world has proven a dysfunctional, dispiriting one. From this disillusion has come the post-modernist vision of the future: from the organised, managed, tidy, rational version of society characterised by all of the visions above, to one that is more disorganised, fuzzy, edgy and disputatious.

This might all seem fine so far, but the post-modern vision has also entailed a profound loss of hope, optimism and belief in change. The future has seemingly gone across the 20th century from being one where everything could be changed, from the nature of mankind's soul to our needs and wants, to believing that nothing could be changed, and that a deep pessimism about the future was what was warranted.

The demise of the modernist account of the future has had one major consequence; it has completely altered the terrain about how we conceive and imagine the future. This is the end of futurology. The science and expertise of seeing the world through the gaze of futurology grew up after the Second World War, at the outset of the Cold War, and at first in the United States, in the work of the massively influential RAND Corporation and the work of Hermann Kahn.

It is this coalescing of forces which gave us much of how people think of future planning today: scenario planning, and 'the three 'Ps and a W': possible, probable and preferred futures along with wildcards, low probability, high impact events. Futurology became how governments, institutions and elites thought of the world, how it would be planned, predictable and understandable.

There are advantages in this approach, in it allows you to collect a lot of information and analyse it. But there are significant limitations. This can be seen in the Hudson Institute's *The Year 2000* published in 1967, which attempted to make sense of the first and second thirds of the 20th century, to delineate the patterns and trends which would shape the final third. While they got many things right such as the rise of China, what they missed is interesting: the limits to economic growth, the rising ecological movement, the changing status of women across the West, and much more.

This was because futurology was about how expert institutions see the world, and wanted to make order and sense of often more complex patterns. And there were also the tendency of those with power and influence to want to see the future as a bigger, better version of today, what has been called linear optimism.

The future of the future isn't anymore about futurology which has been massively undermined by the crisis of modernity along with the rise of the internet. Instead the way in which the future will be more explained will be via the power of stories and the reach and influence of storytellers.

## The Power of Stories

The future belongs to story and storytellers. This in many respects is one of the oldest stories itself. Perhaps the future has always been this way, and just become more explicit and obvious. This taps into the oldest forms of human communication, how stories were told and retold orally before the age of printing and mass communications.

Story is increasingly recognised as being pivotal to how we interpret, make sense, create and see ourselves as active agents in the world. And the notion of story and storytelling is now more and more seen as central to how we think and imagine the future. Even as mainstream and conventional a journal as 'The Economist' has got this, heralding the end of futurology and the future as belonging to storytelling.

There are a number of converging trends in this. There is the widespread acknowledgement of the limits of Enlightenment thinking and in particular the limits of rationalism and 'rational man'. Some may still hanker after the spike of a 'second Enlightenment', but given the plurality of original Enlightenments, now we inhabit the terrain of a post-Enlightenment environment. Human beings in the words of the great philosopher Isaiah Berlin intuitively search for 'the false security of our own symmetrical fantasies' and we have to recognise and counter this tendency.

Story takes us many places. Into the light. And the dark. Into profound choices. And the deepest recesses of the human psyche. Stories aren't always good or used for good. They can be bad or used for bad things. And they can be ambivalent, ambiguous or amoral. When humanity has acted in its most noble, enlightened and liberating ways it has been motivated by story. The uplifting achievements of humanity: the forward march of political democracy, the campaign against third world debt or child poverty, all of these have been animated by positive stories of our potential. Yet there is also a dark side of stories inviting us to limit, repress and dominate each other, seen in the totalitarian dictatorships which disfigured much of the 20th century.

There is always at any point a plurality of stories on offer, that become the dominant stories and counter-stories. What matters at any given point is who is telling the story and how they tell the story. To writers such as Howard Gardner in *Leading Minds* (1996) the stories of an age are all about leadership: Churchill and Britain's 'finest hour', De Gaulle and post-war

France, but then everything is always about leadership in Gardner's world. A subtler take would address the emergence of collective stories; who has voice and influence, and whose stories are marginalised or silenced.

Story does pose a world of more emotional resonance and connection than the world of the RAND Corporation, think tanks and policy wonks. It chimes with the increased understanding we have about how the brain works, the rise of neuroscience and neuropsychology, and how we interpret the world.

This brings us to the final part of this changing environment: the issue of social change. Ideas of how change comes about have also changed dramatically. It has become little more than a tired cliché to say that top-bottom approaches to issues no longer work. The world is much more complicated than that.

There is a gathering sense that the modernist approach, whether Fabian, post-Fabian or free market, left, centre or right didn't work and didn't acknowledge the complexities of what it is to be human. We can also say that the world of policy literacy, of thinking of the world in systems speak and institutional capture, of talking in a post-ideological way of 'evidence based approaches', outputs and outcomes doesn't get us very far. This is an incredibly narrow bandwidth of how we address and assess incredibly challenging issues, and addressing a very technocratic, managerial set of assumptions.

Even after the dreams of the modernist world have been discarded, the avowedly post-modernist, post-ideological approaches have still been in central government and institutions across large parts of the globe, scared to let go. Instead, while realising the limits of government and public agency, they have embraced command and control, and as they have let go of a whole host of macro-issues and retreated from the economic and social contract, moved into a mass of micro-issues in part to justify their legitimacy.

This shift and continuation of government, public agency and action, has to many across the West brought about a wider questioning of centralisation, standardisation and a one size fits all approach. This then takes us into new territory of searching for new ways of addressing the balance between the local, national and international, how you advance universal rights of citizenship and develop certain standards and rights in a more multi-dimensional, multi-national context.

This leads to questions and debates about how change occurs, how ideas emerge, who has voice and influence in public debate and spaces, and the nature of vessels and bodies that people can feel are their own, feel they have a sense of ownership of and which they feel are authentic.

These are huge questions across the West in societies which are less defined by the old notions of class, producers and deference, and are more marked by new forms of status, identity and power.

## The Power of Imagination: Scotlands of the Future

All of these dilemmas and debates have come to the fore in the Scotland of the early years in the 21$^{st}$ century, shaped by our experience of the establishment of the Scottish Parliament, Scotland's place and relationships in the United Kingdom, and our characteristics as a small, northern 'stateless nation'. Our collective journey has aided the changing nature of the UK which may in turn influence and affect Scotland's place and deliberations.

Some people tend to overlook that arguably the most influential book written on Scotland in the last 40 years, Tom Nairn's *The Break-up of Britain* (1977) isn't a book about Scotland on its own. Instead, it is about the reconfiguration of the four nations of the UK, the English dimension, and how external dynamics from European integration to changes in the world economy are reshaping us. This is an argument taken forward in Michael Gardiner's *The Cultural Roots of British Devolution* (2004) which looks at the changes in culture, literature and identities and emergence of a post-British set of identities across these isles. Such a context could lead in a number of directions, culturally, politically and institutionally, but what they point to is to dramatic, far-reaching change.

With all these numerous imponderables this does seem like an exciting, vibrant and challenging time to be living in Scotland. The wider public debate does seem to be very open, evolving and moving somewhere that none of us can be quite sure of at the moment.

Scotland is developing a new collective stories, beginning a conversation about its future, and looking at what issues such as change mean and who can shape and influence them. This book, *ImagiNation: Stories of Scotland's Future*, is a contribution to these debates at a pivotal point in each of these. We can see it in the range, resonance and different voices in this collection.

There are many ingredients in the Scotland of *ImagiNation*: a nation and society at ease with itself and its neighbours, facing up to uncomfortable truths about past, present and future, and looking both inwards with honesty and outwards with generosity. One potent strand which emerges is the yearning for transcending and overcoming tribalism and coming to terms with difference whether it be Highland/Lowland, Protestant/ Catholic, unionist/nationalist, Scottish/English and many more. This is about having the space and willingness for nurturing love and empathy in how we understand each other and accepting that differing opinions and traditions don't necessarily make someone wrong or a lesser person.

Then there is the story of modern Scotland through our personal stories and accounts. This is addressed more and more by Scottish writers both in non-fiction and fiction. It can be found in Ian Jack's newspaper columns in *The Guardian* and his collection, *The Country Formerly Known as Great Britain* (2009) which addresses the issue of memory, remembering and making sense of our loved ones, home towns, and the past whether it be his father's bookshelves, Dunfermline Athletic FC in the 1960s or the local Co-operative Society.

This is a theme taken up in the essays which are contained in this collection and the importance of self-reflection, honesty, and telling collective stories from the sum of individual experiences. James Robertson's opening essay paints a compelling picture of the life journey we travel as the incremental changes cumulate and alter and revise the big picture. These often shape us unnoticed until we stop, look back and take stock, and see 'a new ship built on an old plank'.

A new language and philosophy is required for 21$^{st}$ century Scotland, one which addresses our own unique experience and which is also contributes to the wider global debate about the challenges we face. This has to draw from the past futures we have created, their limitations and possibilities, but pose profoundly that the future is still possible, never closed, never just the conceit of 'the official future' and always open to being made and remade.

This entails learning from the intolerant, inflexible utopian visions of the past, but not as the cynicism of the current age suggests dismissing the utopian impulse and imagination out of hand. As Gregory Claeys wrote in *Searching for Utopia: The History of an Idea* (2011), 'Utopia has been pronounced dead and buried so often'. He then notes its obvious constraints and limitations in that it 'came widely to be perceived as possessing too much Sparta and too little carnival, too much celibacy to too little celebration'. We know only too well that rather austere version of utopia in Scotland, of the elect and select telling us how to live the frugal, disciplined good life, and too little of the vision of play, fun and irreverence.

This touches on Barbara Ehrenreich's idea of 'collective joy', about how human beings need to come together to celebrate, be spontaneous, organise in disorganised, creative ways, and be playful, subversive and challenging in public and as a public. This is an intrinsic part of the collective stories we tell and retell about ourselves, our past, present and future.

Come with us then into the Scotland of the future, or should we say the Scotlands of the future.

# Contributors

**Jane Alexander** grew up in Aberdeen, studied art in Edinburgh and creative writing in Glasgow. She currently works as a creative writing tutor and literature development freelancer, and writes novels and short stories. She has contributed short fiction and creative non-fiction to various magazines and anthologies including *Litro*, *Mslexicampbella*, *The Orphan Leaf Review* and *A Wilder Vein*, and was the recipient of a Scottish Arts Council New Writer's Award.

**Peter Arnott** was born in Glasgow. Since his 1985 debut as a professional writer, he has written plays, songs, cabaret, film and TV scripts. *The Scotsman* named one of his earliest plays, *The Boxer Benny Lynch*, one of Scotland's twenty all-time greatest theatre events. His later work includes *The Breathing House* which won the 2003 TMA Award for Best New Play. He was the National Library of Scotland Writer in Residence from 2008 to 2011. Among his most recent works is an adaptation of Neil M. Gunn's *The Silver Darlings*. He is currently Writer in Residence with the Traverse Theatre and the University of Edinburgh Genomics Forum.

**Bryan Beattie** has written for the stage, TV and radio since 1982, most recently a series of radio dramas for BBC Radio Scotland. He is currently preparing a twenty-six part series on the arts in Scotland for broadcast by the BBC in 2012. He was a columnist for *The Press and Journal* for thirteen years. He was Expert Adviser to two Ministers of Culture in the Scottish Government and Strategic Adviser for the Royal Scottish Academy of Music and Drama. He has led over 200 projects for the cultural consultancy, Creative Services (Scotland) Ltd, and written more reports than is healthy. An album of his songs is due for release in 2011.

**Alan Bissett** is a novelist, playwright and performer who lives in Glasgow. His novels include *Boyracers* **and** *Death of a Ladies Man*, which was shortlisted for a Scottish Arts Council Fiction of the Year prize. His fourth novel, *Pack Men*, will be published in August 2011. His play *Turbo Folk* was shortlisted for Best New Play at the Critics' Awards for Theatre in Scotland 2010. He wrote and performed his 'one-woman' show *The Moira Monologues*, which is now in development with the BBC. The short film which he wrote and narrated, *The Shutdown*, has won awards at several major international film festivals.

**Angus Peter Campbell** is a poet, novelist, journalist, broadcaster and actor. Born in South Uist, he now lives elsewhere, as the Czech emigré writer Vera Linhartova puts it. He graduated in Politics and History from the University of Edinburgh. He was awarded the Bardic Crown in 2001, the same year he was given a Creative Scotland Award. In 2004 his Gaelic novel, *An Oidhche Mus Do Sheòl Sinn* was short-listed for the Saltire Society Book of the Year, and in 2006 was also voted by the readers of *The List* magazine into the Top Ten of the Best-Ever Books Written in Scotland. He was nominated by BAFTA Scotland as lead actor in the Gaelic film *Seachd*. In August 2010 he published his first novel in English – *Archie and the North Wind*, and a new collection of his poetry, *Aibisidh* – including the *Stuagh-Mara* published here – was published in July 2011.

**Bill Duncan** was born and raised in Fife before moving to Dundee. He is Head of English in an Angus Secondary school. His fiction, non-fiction and poetry have been widely published in magazines and newspapers, with fiction broadcast on BBC Radio 3 and 4. Bill's ongoing exploration of real and imaginary Scottish maritime cultures extends across an ever-widening range of media. Previous projects include fiction (*The Smiling School for Calvinists*) and non-fiction (*The Wee Book of Calvin*). *The Hirta Portfolio* is a collaboration based on his poems and Susan Wilson's etchings, while thehaar (www.thehaar.org.uk) is an ambitious web-based environment created with artist and designer Andy Rice with contributions from a range of musicians. His work has been performed at Dundee Rep and he recently collaborated on the *Ballads of the Book* project.

**Ronald Frame** was born in Glasgow and educated at university there and in Oxford. He has written thirteen works of fiction and is an award-winning TV and radio scriptwriter. He has received international recognition for his short stories about the fictitious spa town of Carnbeg. These have been published as a book of short stories, broadcast on BBC Radio 4, and were published in *The Herald* over a six-month period followed by a further six months in *The Scotman*. In 1984 he won the first Betty Trask prize for fiction. His 1999 novel, *The Lantern Bearers*, was longlisted for the Man Booker Prize and won the 2000 Saltire Society Award for Scottish Book of the Year. In 2005 it was named one of the 100 Best Scottish Books. In 2010 he published his first novel in eight years, *Unwritten Secrets*.

**David Greig** was born in Edinburgh in 1969 and brought up in Nigeria, later returning to Edinburgh before studying drama at Bristol University. He chose to pursue directing and writing, rather than acting, and co-founded Suspect Culture theatre group in Glasgow in 1990 to produce collaborative, experimental theatre work. He is a prolific playwright, whose works include *San Diego* and his version of Euripides' *The Bacchae*, both of which premiered at the Edinburgh International Festival. *Dunsinane* is his most recent play, an imagined sequel to Macbeth which was commissioned by the Royal Shakespeare Company. He is dramaturg of the National Theatre of Scotland and has also been commissioned by the Royal Court and National Theatre.

**Gerry Hassan** was born in Dundee and has lived in Glasgow for nearly twenty years. He is a writer, commentator, broadcaster and policy analyst on a range of issues. He has written and edited over a dozen books on Scotland, the UK, politics, policy and ideas. His latest books include *Radical Scotland: Arguments for Self-Determination* and *The Modern SNP: From Protest to Power*. He is a Demos Associate and headed up their Scotland 2020 and Glasgow 2020 projects which led to the books *Scotland 2020: Hopeful Stories for a Northern Nation* and *The Dreaming City: Glasgow 2020 and the Power of Mass Imagination*. He is a regular *Scotsman* columnist, Open Democracy commentator and blogger. He is head of A Scottish Wave of Change project. His writing and research can be found at: www.gerryhassan.com

**Sam Irving** was born in Dundee. He has written poetry since his schooldays but this is his first submission for publication. He looks forward to holding the book in his hands, showing his mum a copy, and seeing it in bookshops. It might inspire him to share more of his work.

**Helen Jackson** lives in Edinburgh, having moved there in 1998 after falling in love with the city during a weekend break. She is a member of the critically acclaimed spoken word collective Writers' Bloc, who perform regularly in the Capital. She is also a Scottish BAFTA-nominated animation director.

**William Letford** is a writer and poet living in Stirling. Aged eleven, his primary school teacher sent one of his poems to Roger McGough, who wrote back to William with the advice 'KEEP WRITING'. Now he combines his job as a roofer with studying at Glasgow University's Creative Writing Masters course. He was named by the Scottish Book Trust as one of the 2008 New Writers and was recently awarded the Edwin Morgan travel bursary to allow him to travel to Italy to help restore a medieval village and write poetry. He also recently received an SQA Star Award. He has been published in *Discovering a Comet* and *More Micro-Fiction*.

**Kirsty Logan** is twenty-seven and lives in Glasgow with her girlfriend. Her short fiction has been published in around eighty anthologies and literary magazines, and broadcast on BBC Radio 4. In 2009 she graduated from Glasgow University's Creative Writing MLitt; over the following year she won the New Writers Award from the Scottish Book Trust, the Gillian Purvis Award, and third place in the Bridport Prize. She is now working on her first novel, *Little Dead Boys*, and a short story collection, *The Rental Heart and Other Fairytales*. Say hello at kirstylogan. com.

**Allan Massie** was born in Singapore. After graduating from Cambridge University he embarked on a career in teaching. He was Creative Writing Fellow at Edinburgh, Glasgow and Strathclyde Universities. He is a Fellow of the Royal Society of Literature. He has written extensively for newspapers, and has been fiction reviewer for *The Scotsman* since 1976. He has written nearly thirty books, including twenty novels. These include the acclaimed *Imperial Sequence* – a series of historical novels set in the Roman Empire. His non-fiction includes works about Muriel Spark, Colette and Byron. He lives in Selkirk.

**Donald McKenzie** was born in West Lothian and now lives in Inverness. As a mature student he studied drawing and painting at Grays School of Art in Aberdeen, followed by postgraduate studies at Duncan of Jordanstone in Dundee, attaining an MFA in 2001. Donald continues to make and exhibit art and also has had writing published locally. He received a Highly Commended in the National Gallery Creative Writing Competition in 2007, and was placed third in the Neil M. Gunn Writing Contest in 2008.

**Mark McNay** was born in a former mining village in Scotland. Aged eighteen, he moved to England and has had a variety of jobs, including factory work, building work and window cleaning. He graduated with distinction from the University of East Anglia's Creative Writing course in 2003. In 2007, his first novel *Fresh* won the Arts Foundation Prize for New Fiction and the Saltire Society First Book Award. His second novel is *Under Control*. He lives in Norwich, where he is currently working on his third novel.

**Rob Miller** has been involved in the Glasgow comic scene for five years, contributing to the anthology title *Khaki Shorts* and working with John Miller (and latterly Adam J. Smith) on their related small press publications *Super Tales* and *Atomic Society*. Based at Hope Street Studios, he is currently collecting local artists under the *Braw Books* imprint whilst undertaking art assist duties for Frank Quitely.

**Raman Mundair** is a writer and artist. She was born in India and lives and works in Scotland. Mundair is the author of *A Choreographer's Cartography, Lovers, Liars, Conjurers and Thieves* and *The Algebra of Freedom*. She is a Rolex Mentor and Protégé Award nominee, a Robert Louis Stevenson Award winner and was identified recently by the BBC/Royal Court Theatre as one of the 'next generation of promising new writers in Britain'. *The Independent* newspaper wrote in a review of her work 'Raman Mundair is a rare breed: a poet whose writing works on the page and the stage. Her readings reveal the secret music of the poem... Mundair is literature at its best: thoughtful, provocative and sharp.'

**Rona Munro** was born in Aberdeen. She started writing professionally in 1981, and writes for theatre, film, TV and radio. Her film credits include the script for *Ladybird, Ladybird*, directed by Ken Loach. Among her TV scripts is a series of *Doctor Who* and *Rehab* directed by Antonia Bird. Her recent credits include the screenplay for *Oranges and Sunshine* directed by Jim Loach, *Little Eagles* for the RSC and *Pandas* for The Traverse Theatre.

**Nulsh** was born in Midlothian and now lives in Glasgow. He started his career as a freelance illustrator, cartoonist and animator in 1987. He drew the script *Bush Doctor*, written by Alan Grant, and has contributed to magazines such as *Northern*

*Lightz, Freak, Soft Secrets, Dangerous Ink, Instant* and *Layer Zero*. Most of his original scripts are self-published, such as *Hen's Teeth*. For more information about his work, visit www.nulsh.com

**Morna Pearson** is from Elgin and currently lives in Edinburgh. Her first full professional production was *Distracted* at The Traverse Theatre in 2006. *Distracted* won the Meyer-Whitworth Award and was nominated for a CATS Award. Her other plays include *Elf Analysis* (Oran Mor), *McBeth's Pets* (BBC Radio Scotland), *Side Effects* (BBC Radio 3/Bona Broadcasting) and *The Company Will Overlook a Moment of Madness* (adaptation) (NTS/Oran Mor).

**Tom Pow** was born in Edinburgh and studied at St Andrews University. He lives in Dumfries, where he is an Honorary Senior Research Fellow at Glasgow University's Crichton Campus. Four of his five full collections – *Rough Seas, The Moth Trap, Landscapes and Legacies* and *Dear Alice – Narratives of Madness* – have won Scottish Arts Council Book Awards. *In the Becoming – New and Selected Poems* was published in 2009. As a writer for children, he won a further SAC Book Award. He has also written a travel book and radio plays. In 2000 he became Scotland's first Virtual Writer in Residence for the Scottish Library Association, and between 2001 and 2003 was the first Writer in Residence at the Edinburgh International Book Festival. In 2007 he received a Creative Scotland Award from the Scottish Arts Council for a project exploring dying villages throughout Europe.

**Allan Radcliffe** was born in Perth and now lives in Edinburgh. His short stories have appeared in *New Writing Scotland, Markings, Celtic View, Gutter* and *Elsewhere*. He won a Scottish Book Trust New Writers Award in 2009 and is currently working on his first novel, *Buttons for Eyes*.

**Michael Rigg** was born in Cornwall, went to school in Morayshire, worked as a film editor in London and has lived in Glasgow since 1978. He is a member of the Triratna Buddhist Order in which he is known as Shantiketu. He has published a book about using computer games in education as well as the occasional poem and short story in magazines such as the Cambridge-based *Urthona* and the American journal *The Formalist*.

**James Robertson** was born in Kent, but grew up in Bridge of Allan, Stirlingshire, from the age of six. After graduating in history from Edinburgh University, he worked in various jobs before becoming a full-time writer. His first book, a collection of short stories, was published in 1991. Since then he has published more than twenty books for adults and children, including *The Testament of Gideon Mack*, which was longlisted for the Man Booker Prize. From 1993 to 1995 he was writer in residence at Brownsbank Cottage, Hugh MacDiarmid's former home near Biggar. He is a co-founder of, and editor and contributing author to, the Scots language children's imprint Itchy Coo. He set up the pamphlet-publishing imprint Kettillonia in 1999. His latest novel *And The Land Lay Still* was named Saltire Society Scottish Book of the Year in 2010.

**Cynthia Rogerson** is a Californian living in Ross-shire. Her first novel, *Upstairs in the Tent*, was published in 2001. Her short stories and poems have been short-listed for competitions, anthologized, published in literary magazines and broadcast on BBC radio. In 2008 she won the V S Pritchett Short Story Award. *Love Letters from my Death-Bed* was nominated for the Saltire Prize and the Scottish Arts Council Prize. Her most recent novel, *I Love You, Goodbye*, was nominated for Best Scottish Book of the Year 2011. She is director of the Moniack Mhor Arvon Writers Centre in Inverness-shire.

**Ciaran Slavin** is a freelance digital artist and character designer. He has been involved in illustration and the production of comics since 1990, and graduated in Animation and Digital Art from the University of Paisley in 2005.

**David Tomei** is a freelance illustrator based in Glasgow. He studied Illustration at Glasgow Metropolitan and has been working hard on his craft ever since. He lives in Coatbridge with his family.

**Alice Walsh** was born in Dublin and has lived in Perth since 1983 with her partner and their two children. She began writing short fiction and poetry nine years ago after attending a creative writing class in Perth. She is a member of Perth's Soutar Writers Group. She has worked as a cleaner, archaeologist, meter reader, and since 1991 for an environmental charity. Other stories have appeared in *Chapman*, *Shortbread* (online) and local Perthshire publications.

**Alan Warner** was born in 1964 and grew up in Connel, near Oban. He is seen by many critics as one of the most exciting voices in contemporary Scottish literature. In 2003, *Granta* magazine nominated him as one of the twenty Best Young British Novelists. His novels include the highly acclaimed *Morvern Callar* (winner of a Somerset Maugham Award), *These Demented Lands*, *The Sopranos* (winner of the Saltire Society Scottish Book of the Year), *The Man Who Walks* and *The Worms Can Carry Me to Heaven*. His most recent novel, *The Stars in the Bright Sky*, was published in 2010 and long-listed for the Man Booker Prize. His forthcoming novel, *Dead Man's Pedal*, will be published in May 2012.

**Chris Watson** was born in Edinburgh and grew up in Stirling. He graduated with a BA in Drawing and Painting from Glasgow School of Art, with part of his studies taken at the School of the Art Institute of Chicago, USA. Chris also has an MA in Sequential Illustration and Design from Brighton University. Chris' award winning artwork features in books and magazines, and has been commissioned for fashion and music labels. Clients include *Cycling Active*, *The Guardian*, Savoy Jazz and Penguin.

**Benjamin Werdmuller** is based in Edinburgh and California. He creates digital things for a living, most recently as Chief Technical Officer for Latakoo, a web company that allows TV and video professionals to send video quickly. Previously, he co-founded Elgg, a popular open source social networking platform, and he has spoken internationally about social networking technology. Writing is his first love.

**Alan Wilkins'** plays include *The Nest* and *Carthage Must be Destroyed* for The Traverse Theatre. As well as his own writing he has also worked as a playwright tutor with a multitude of groups, including school pupils, university students, young offenders, adult offenders and psychiatric patients. He has worked all over Scotland as well as in Lichtenstein, The Netherlands and Russia.

# Acknowledgements

This book is the product of many hands, contributions and visions. It is impossible to thank every person who has played a part in *Imagination: Stories of Scotland's Future*, but the biggest thanks go to all of the writers who have created such a varied, vibrant and diverse collection. Thanks also to all the entrants to our national story competition. The work of seven of them – Jane Alexander, Sam Irving, Helen Jackson, Donald McKenzie, Michael Rigg, Alice Walsh and Ben Werdmuller – appears in this book.

This project would not have been possible without the existence and support of A Scottish Wave of Change, a national programme of events and activities on Scotland's future through the idea of story that sits as part of the Cultural Olympiad. Many thanks to all those who have made A Scottish Wave of Change possible, the numerous events, initiatives and stories. In particular a big thank you to George Thomson and Alison Bielecka at Volunteer Development Scotland and Jaine Lumsden at Creative Scotland.

Numerous people gave invaluable advice to make this book happen. Ron Grosset at Waverley Books has been a tower of inspiration and enthusiastic support of this project from its beginning. He has tirelessly assisted in pointing this project in the right direction while not once questioning or doubting its potential. We are indebted to his input.

Also, Richard Walker and Susan Flockhart at *The Sunday Herald* for their encouragement and support of the national story competition; and Marc Lambert at the Scottish Book Trust has given an enormous amount of time, experience and encouragement throughout, including as a judge of the national story competition.

James Grant and Vincent Deighan at Hope Street Studios in Glasgow helped identify graphic artists and writers and Prof. Christopher Murray of the University of Dundee gave advice on the world of the comic book community. David Greig and Katherine Mendelsohn at the Traverse Theatre gave invaluable support and encouragement in bringing together a range of some of Scotland's finest playwrights as part of the project. Professor Willy Maley of the University of Glasgow gave generous and helpful advice that helped guide the content.

Gavin Wallace and Aly Barr at Creative Scotland, and Marion Sinclair at Publishing Scotland also gave us their professional advice and support at important points.

James Robertson's essay (slightly amended for the present volume) first appeared in *The Sunday Herald* on 1 August 2010 under the title Who Are The Scots? We are grateful for their permission to use the essay in this collection.

Apologies to those we've missed from this list – we appreciated your help.

**For Big Sky Press**
Huge thanks to Fiona Fowler for co-ordinating the project, giving assistance and being a source of calm confidence throughout this process. Jane Wilde has typeset and designed all aspects of the book with talent and patience, and Adrian Lear gave insightful advice and suggestions from the start.

Thanks to Jean Urquhart for the most sensible advice we received at the outset of this project, but still went on to totally ignore; to the whole team at Creative Services (Scotland) Ltd for pitching in with whatever was needed; and to Emer and the family for their usual patience and tolerance.

o o o

The publisher gratefully acknowledges the following for permission to use the copyright material:
An extract from *Scottish Journey* by Edwin Muir, 1935, published by Mainstream.
An extract from *Hermless* by Michael Marra.
*To Know Him Is To Love Him* Words and Music by Phil Spector © 1958, Reproduced by permission of EMI Music Publishing Ltd/Abkco Music Inc, London W8 5SW
An extract from *Caledonia* by Dougie MacLean, Limetree Arts and Music, 1982.
An extract from *The Highwayman* by Alfred Noyes, The Society of Authors as the literary representative of the Estate of Alfred Noyes.

The text featured on the cover is from Jules Verne's *The Underground City* (1877), a novel set in a future Scotland envisioned as a classless, technological utopia. The French author believed Scotland had lost its capacity to imagine progress.
'For you I was the flame. Love is a losing game' is an extract from the Amy Winehouse song *Love is a Losing Game* from the album *Back to Black*, 2006, Island Records.

# About A Scottish Wave of Change

A Scottish Wave of Change is part of the Cultural Olympiad – which addresses the future, stories and change. It is about aiding and encouraging discussion, stories, creativity and hope in a mass imagination project, opening up and democratising the future.

The project has a national remit – using the Olympic and Paralympic values to begin an exploration of the values, hopes and aspirations people would like to see in the Scotland of the future. It has significant community projects, working in Govan, Dundee and Lochgilphead developing local futures contributing to a different national future, while supporting a group of young people to sail around Scotland – creating stories of the future. All of its activities are about supporting, identifying and nurturing the idea of change through stories, imagination, connection and conversation which aids bringing about the Scotland of the future.

More details on A Scottish Wave of Change can be found at:
www.imaginingscotland.com

More information on People Making Waves and the Cultural Olympiad can be found at: www.peoplemakingwaves.org.uk

**LOTTERY FUNDED**

**LOTTERY FUNDED**

People Making Waves is part of The Scottish Project, which will create a cultural legacy from the London 2012 Olympic and Paralympic Games in Scotland. It is supported by Legacy Trust UK and by the National Lottery through Creative Scotland.